Pierre Bensusan

Guitar book

jacket : « Fleury's Garden », aquarelle by Denise Cornu

Published in English by

7777 W. BLUEMOUND RD. P.O. BOX 13819 MILWAUKEE, WI 53213

© & ℗ 1985 par Pierre Bensusan, P.O. Box 411, Mill Valley CA. 94941, USA
TOUS DROITS D'EXÉCUTION, DE REPRODUCTION ET D'ARRANGEMENT RÉSERVÉS POUR TOUS PAYS

ISBN 0-88188-620-3

ACKNOWLEDGMENTS

Written in collaboration with Doatea BENSUSAN. I thank her for her help and inspiration in this work as for everything else.
Loïc TRÉHIN *(engravings, aquarelles, technical and artistic photography, layout, graphic conception and technical realization).*
René COSTE *(musical notation and tablature transcription)*
and Mike VOGEL *(translation).*
I also thank my parents Renée and George very deeply...

Special thanks to :

Anne Marie MARTINS
Kathy HORTON
Philippe STEGER *(photography)*
Denise CORNU *(oil)*
Patrick ALEXANDRE *(illustrations, technical sketches, key of tablature and harmonics symbols)*
Vincen CORNU *(drawings and illustrations for recipes)*
Gérard REBOURS *(advice and documentation)*
Gérard CHARNOZ *(advice)*
Frédéric LEIBOVITZ & Jean-Michel GALLOIS-MONTBRUN
(for their kind authorization to use titles belonging to CEZAME/ARGILE Publishing Co.)

Roberto AUSSEL

Steve ARMSTRONG
Jacques BARBERI *(photography)*
CLADDAGH RECORDS (Dublin)
Daniel CARIOU *(photography)*
Gérard CORNU *(poetry)*
Maddy CORNU
Dave EVANS
Bob GILES *(notes)*
Nicky GYGGER *(photography)*
Bruce HARRIS *(wood engraving)*
JAZZ-HOT Magazine *(Paris)*
Maureen KEARNEY
Bill KEITH
Yvon KERVINIO *(photography)*
Lisa LAW *(photography)*
Hélène LE LUHERNE *(layout)*
LEDUC Publishing Co. (Paris)
François LEMONNIER
LIBERATION Newspaper (Paris)
Jennifer LINEHAN *(photography)*
Georges LOWDEN
Colm MITCHELL
Michèle NEDELEC *(photography)*
Francine PAILLET *(poetry)*
Lawrence PERQUIS *(photography)*
Henri PICHETTE *(photography)*
Billy RILEY *(photography)*
Jean-Marie REDON
Eric SCHOENBERG
Josiane TRÉHIN
Irène YOUNG *(photography)*
Georges WINSTON
Philippe ZANI

as well as all those who gave me their valuable encouragment and support.

PREFACE

Over the past 20 years, there has been a steady stream of works written about and for the guitar, in the form of books, methods, and scores ; each has specialized in one area, offering historical information, notes on guitar players or guitar makers, or simply pieces.

Today, I have the pleasure of presenting Pierre Bensusan's « Guitar Book ».

This book is the result of six years of thought and research. It is also the joint effort of a group of people who have managed to write not only a guitar book, but an art book thought out for guitarists while reaching beyond their universe.

How can I describe its contents, considering that the information it gives is so vast ?

It contains explanations, from the workings of the hands to suggestions for specific exercises designed to help acquire correct technique, definitions of terminology employed in music and for the guitar, and suggestions for awakening and improving one's own sense of musicality, not to mention all the works composed, transcribed or arranged by Pierre Bensusan to support the advice he offers.

I would like to place particular emphasis on the use of different tunings, of which guitarists are very apprehensive, but which lead us to improve our inner ear in the same way as we develop our knowledge of the guitar neck.

This book can also help us sharpen our intellectual and sensorial perception. It is sprinkled with poems, illustrations, reproductions of art works, even recipes.

Given this amount of material, the reader will want to read this book attentively, over and over again. Though the book may seem disorganized at first glance, the author designed it that way as an invitation to delve into each idea suggested, creating a veritable dialogue between the book and its reader.

All that is left for me to do is to congratulate Pierre Bensusan for having taken the initiative to condense all his thoughts in his « Guitar Book », which I wish a very long life, as well as his highly original music which opens up pathways to a new world of sound.

Roberto AUSSEL.

« I prefer night, when it is lit by a thin crescent of a moon being born, because I love all things that have a future ».

Om Kalsoum

to my wife

INTRODUCTION

This book is not exactly a method ; rather it is a collection of music intended for guitarists who are already familiar with the instrument, whether it be the steel string or classical nylon string guitar. The order in which the pieces are presented is relatively progressive, although that order does not necessarily have to be followed systematically. The book's eclectic nature stems from the fact that it contains many of my first adaptations and short compositions, alongside pieces that are much more recent. Written music seems « fixed », while played music very often undergoes transformation. That explains the occasional divergences between the scores presented in the book and my recordings (see list of recordings, pg. 182).

The glossary can be consulted at any time for answers to technical, interpretative, or terminological questions. The answers are of a general order and are based on my research into and experience with different tunings. As I have always been particularly interested in the resonances and melodic wealth of traditional music containing drone lines, I decided at an early stage to concentrate on open tunings, especially the tuning : *D-A-D-G-A-D*. The sympathetic vibrations produced among the strings expand sonorities, which are further enriched by tuning the lowest string a whole step lower. The result is freedom of the left hand, which can then be devoted more to melody and ornaments. Moreover, while this type of tuning makes the key of *D* extremely attractive, it obviously takes nothing away from modulations or playing in other keys.

The use of open tunings brings new mechanisms into play, creating the possibility of enhancing technique, harmonic color, and consequently, the music itself. The only disadvantage it presents is in upsetting habits acquired by the ear and the fingers (new positions and wider stretches). Opening oneself up to different techniques is not a question of challenging one's basic precepts. Moreover, that which is inhabitual is not necessarily difficult.

This book is intended to bolster the player who feels limited for reasons of bodily configuration or flexibility. When working out a technique, of whatever nature, it is essential to be as musical as possible. Technique consists of improvements and increased assuredness as well as of more mobile concepts that constantly undergo change.

In any case, stepping beyond the written word and note, the charm of pure sounds elicits a reaction even before they are named. And while the fact of turning towards one's instrument sometimes feels as unsettling as walking out of a warm house on a cold, stormy night, it can also feel as comforting as settling down to make hot chocolate and cookies, which is not always easy.

The Author

GLOSSARY

AMPLIFICATION

« Right now, I think that amplification is perfect. Orchestration has become more interesting than the unamplified tradition ».

Leo BROUWER.

At the time when amplification did not exist, instruments such as the lute, the baroque guitar, and the classical guitar were designed to produce a sufficient amount of sound to be played solo or in small groups. Concerts were also given in appropriate places, such as churches, amphitheaters, and more recently, Italianate theaters (designed according to elaborate acoustical principles) and salons for small groups of listeners. There exists a « classical » tradition, whose aim is to stick to the acoustics of music as they were produced in the past, and to interpret more modern pieces with the same attitude. Aside from the fact that musical instrument building techniques have not ceased to progress, it now seems difficult to avoid using any form of amplification in halls built to hold larger audiences, and whose acoustics are often designed in terms of changing techniques and musical criteria. At present, the quality and precision of amplification make it possible to reproduce acoustic sounds with consummate fidelity and discretion.

Conversation with George LOWDEN, *(guitar maker of Northern Ireland)*

– P.B. : *Is amplification a problem ? Can it be solved ?*

– G.L. : *Amplification is a problem, but it can be solved. The only problem is price and portability. The best loud reproduction of an acoustic guitar is achieved by using a superior quality mike, along with a very large and fullrange P.A. system. Unfortunately, this is difficult for most musicians, and therefore a compromise must be reached. A mike or a normal transducer can be used through an instrument amplifier, but the problem here is in achieving good volume without feedback. Using a pickup which is mounted inside the bridge is the obvious answer, because this type of transducer is not susceptible to feedback, and therefore the amplifier can be turned up to achieve good volume. However, these pickups vary quite a bit in terms of the actual tone quality produced. The best ones are still very acoustic in nature. We had some problems with the first pickups we produced with this type of system, for although the volume and tonal quality was excellent, there were occasionally some string balance problems. The first pickups seemed to be very sensitive to their exact position in relation to the strings. However, with some adjustments to the pickup design, this problem is rarely evident now. But the whole area of acoustic pickup design is constantly under review, and no doubt new designs will be forthcoming.*

Note : as one of many examples of amplification techniques, this combination of three sound sources :

– a pickup, installed under the bridge, picks up high frequencies and produces a rather crystalline timbre.
– a sound hole pickup, which is closer to the top of the fingerboard, reproduces more faithfully the medium-bass frequencies while tempering the treble notes and producing a sound that is richer overall.
– a microphone placed before the guitar, between the sound hole and the top of the fingerboard reproduces acoustic sound, in addition to the direct reproduction provided by the two pickups, and unifies the sound in the listening room.

By coloring each of the three signals and mixing them, the guitarist produces by himself a sound that is more dynamic and richer in nuances depending on the musical ideas and equipment at his disposal. (Guitar amplifire, equalizer, pre-amp for pickups, reverb, echo, various effect pedals, volume pedal, etc.).

ARPEGGIATED CHORDS

« Arpeggiating a chord means playing the notes one after another rather than at the same time, in such a way as to form a complete chord at the end ».

Théorie complète de la musique, 1st volume, J. CHAILLEY and H. CHALLAN, Editions LEDUC (Paris).

The arpeggiated chord is preceded on the staff by the sign ⸸ . It is generally played from the bass to the treble.

interpretation :
1) preceding the downbeat (pickup), that is, the last note is on the beat :

written :

2) on the downbeat, that is, the first note is on the beat :

An arrow pointing downwards indicates that the arpeggio is to be played from the treble to the bass.

ex :

 etc

It would be too long to illustrate all types of arpeggios and their variations, in terms of fingerings and rhythms, all the more so, because this involves both the harmony and construction of chords. Nevertheless, the present collection offers many examples of arpeggiated chords. In many cases, their interpretation will be left up to the player *(see arpeggio exercises, pg. 46)*.

When using this technique, the guitarist's right hand is like the harpist's, playing chords by plucking the strings as if the chord were a broken necklace and the notes a string of pearls that one can hear falling distinctly, one by one. (See ATTACKS and ARPEGGIOS).

ARPEGGIOS

In the classical meaning of the term, the arpeggio is a series of notes that gives the ear the impression of a chord.

There are several types of arpeggios, including melodic, broken, and harmonic arpeggios.

- The arpeggio is *melodic* when the notes make up a melody which is perfectly in keeping with a specific rhythm.

ex. :

F chord   melodic arpeggio of the chord

- The *broken* arpeggio is a melodic arpeggio in which the notes are played in an irregular order.

ex. :

broken arpeggio

- In the *harmonic* arpeggio, the notes are held (creating an effect similar to the sustaining pedal on a piano). When the notes are played in the regular order of the chord, the effect is known as an *arpeggiated chord*.

The word *arpeggio* has a broader meaning in guitar playing. It designates any series of notes played in a precise order and in a repetitive manner.

Due to the very placement of the strings, the anatomy and action of the fingers, the guitar is particularly well adapted to playing arpeggios *(see ARPEGGIATED CHORDS and arpeggio exercises, pg. 46)*.

ATTACKS

Throughout the pieces in this collection, the right hand is exercised in order to develop the use of the bare fingers without using flat or thumb picks. By developing coordination and independent movement, the player can avoid having to specialize in any one style of playing. More extensive right hand technique contributes to the personality of the sound produced, and thus, total musical expression, through the tackling of all new demands with equal ease.

All five fingers of the right hand are used to produce the sound by attacking the strings.

Generally speaking, the thumb is used for the three bass strings, whereas the index, ring, and middle fingers are placed over the other strings. The little finger, while less powerful due to its size and position on the hand, should not be ignored. It is logically used in strummed or arpeggiated chords when more than four strings are played. In that case, however, the thumb can also be slid consecutively over the first two strings of the chord.

There are even times when the index, middle, and ring fingers play the bass strings while the thumb plays the upper strings.

When several notes are to be played in succession on any one string, the fingers must be chosen in a logical order, avoiding the use of the same finger twice consecutively. The thumb, is as muscular as all the other fingers combined. The flexibility of its joints and nail, with respect to the strings, enables it to slide over them and play many times in rapid succession. On the contrary, in *rest stroke*, in *picking*, in arpeggios and melodic lines, the other fingers alternate over one or more strings. The following are the main combinations possible :

– *index finger (i), middle finger (m), ring finger (a), middle, index, middle, etc., or abbreviated : i, m, a, m, i, m...*[1]
– *a, m, i, a, m, i...*
– *i, m, a, i, m, a... (see exercises, pg. 86)*

In the case where the thumb is used to play the two lowest strings, the index on the third, and the middle finger, the ring finger, and the little finger on the three highest strings :

– *i, m, a, pt, a, m, i... (pt : little finger)* [1]
– *i, m, a, pt, i, m, a, pt, i...*
– *pt, a, m, i, pt, a, m, i, pt...*
– *m, a, pt, a, m, a, pt, a...*
– *m, a, pt, m, a, pt, m...*
– *pt, a, m, a, pt, a, m, a, pt...*

Another technique is derived from that used for ancient instruments (such as the *gittern, vihuela,* and *lute*) whereby the plectrum is not used, making it possible to play solos with ease, even if the thumb is occasionally required for the bass notes. That technique is called *figueta* :

The thumb *(p)*, alternates with the index or middle finger, and sometimes even the ring finger, over a single string and from one string to the next :

[1] *p, i, p, m, etc* making free use of any of those combinations (*see exercises, pg. 86*).

– The succession of fingers on the strings
– their attack
– the use of the flesh, the nail, and their combined timbres
– the place where the fingers touch the strings are all determining factors, broadening the range of nuances and the impact of the player's goal.

[1] abreviations for finger indications are based on the French names for the different fingers as they appear in the scores (following) :
    p (pouce) = *thumb*
    i (index) = *index finger*
    m (majeur) = *middle finger*
    a (annulaire) = *ring finger*
    pt (petit doigt) = *little finger*

Every guitarist develops an attitude depending on the shape and size of his instrument, his anatomy, the music he plays, and his technique. Thus, all these factors, whose purpose and interrelations should occasionally be reiterated, ultimately blend into a coherent attitude which he takes for granted.

In the case where the bend in the elbow is blocked against the angle in the upper part of the guitar body, the hand moves forward and is placed next to the sound hole.

When the forearm rests, almost in the middle, in the curve of the sidewalls, the hand falls directly in front of the soundhole (a common position in classical guitar playing).

Whatever the manner of placing the arm, the forearm, and the wrist, the guitarist should ensure that no muscular effort is added and that the articulations are not frozen (especially that of the wrist). This allows for greater choice and clarity in attacks and phrasing.

While some guitarists play without using their nails, developing a specific sound with the fleshy part of the fingers, others choose to play using their nails and to *balance* the sound produced using the nails with that produced by the flesh.

● *Picking* : the rounded fingers *hook* the strings in an upward motion. The angle of the finger with respect to the string varies depending on the timbre and volume desired.

A bit of advice : Avoid resting the little finger on the body of the guitar. While it stabilizes the hand, it ultimately becomes incapable of supporting itself and moving freely along the strings. Moreover, it causes a needless contraction of the forearm and the fingers, making them dependent upon that *crutch*.

● *Rest stroke* (Spanish : *apoyando*) : the finger brushes past the string and rests on the string below. The string vibrates almost vertically (*perpendicularly to the fret board*) and the sound, softened by the flesh of the finger, increases in volume.

Although the *rest stroke* is more commonly used when playing guitars with nylon strings, many players use the stroke with steel strings. In that case, the energy of the attack must be controlled to keep the strings from grazing one another.

Generally speaking, as the same finger is never used twice consecutively, it is advisable to alternate between the index and middle fingers. However, the fact that the middle finger is larger than the index could cause slight destabilization of the hand. For that reason – and this is only a minor detail – some players prefer alternating the index finger with the ring finger, because their equivalent lengths balance the fingering.

Here are some possible combinations :

– *i, m, i, m, i...*
– *i, a, i, a, i...*
– *m, a, m, a, m...*
– *m, i, m, i, m...*
– *a, i, a, i, a...*
– *a, m, a, m, a...*

Other players use the three fingers to spread out the effort and increase the number of combinations.

While the thumb pick makes it possible to attack the strings more easily and even replace the flat pick in the performance of solos, it is better to use it only occasionally or not at all, in order to achieve a sound with greater nuance and warmth, as produced using the bare thumb (*see THUMB PICK*).

The timbre also varies depending on the spot at which the strings are attacked. The closer one plays to the top of the fingerboard, where the strings are more flexible, the sound is softer, whereas it becomes incisive and more powerful closer to the bridge, where the strings are more taut.

The player is encouraged to look for his own variations in timbre, by playing continuous arpeggios in which the hand moves slowly along the strings, from the end of the fret board towards the bridge, and so forth. He should avoid applying too much force or stiffness to the fingers, because that can be heard in the music. The fingers should be allowed to fall on the strings under their own weight, leaving them their natural relaxation time between each attack.

Another way to modify the resonance of the bass strings consists in damping them while playing, by allowing the outer edge of the palm to rest on them, weightless. This is easier to do with the pick, using the little finger as a fulcrum on the table.

I hope the pieces in this book give the reader the desire and occasion to develop ease in the right hand as well as the curiosity to try out new combinations of fingerings, nuances, attacks, and other techniques altogether. Among flamenco guitarists, for example Ramon MONTOYA, SABICAS, Paco DE LUCIA, and Paco PENA, use of the right hand is rich. The same holds true for many other musicians who have developed individual styles, such as Lenny BREAU, Leo BROUWER, Egberto GISMONTI, Ralph TOWNER, Stanley JORDAN, Michael HEDGES, Wes MONTGOMERY, Roberto AUSSEL, and Cacho TIRAO...

In order for the right hand to be able to deliver soft, heavy, brilliant, light, fiery, and velvety sounds, in alternation, it must remain relaxed and free, and offer the sensation – by its very physical, sensitive, and sensual action – of rendering music's *invisible* qualities.

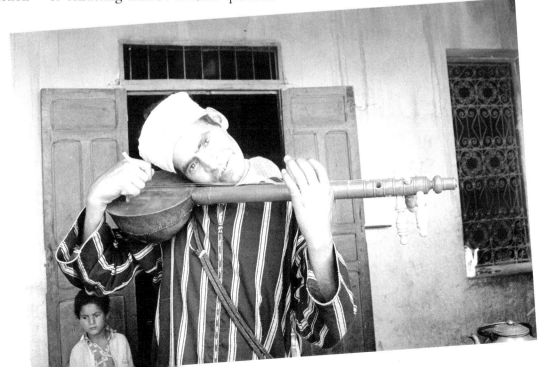

NAIL CARE
(according to the method devised by Michael Bellmont and Steve Armstrong)

Even when nails receive normal care – filing, polishing, and lacquering – they wear and break more readily when playing on steel strings. The following preparation, using a very strong glue and baking soda, builds up nails that are fragile or that grow incorrectly. Unlike artificial nails, this nail coating does not alter tactile sensitivity. It fits all shapes of nails, and when applied carefully, it lasts longer.

INGREDIENTS
- solvent (or acetone)
- a pin
- strong glue (super glue, crazy glue...)
- a nail file (very fine)
- baking soda (bicarbonate of soda, stored in a small hermetically sealed box)
- a small brush
- a polishing file or extra fine sandpaper
- neutral lacquer or hardener.

1. Clean the nail with solvent.
2. a. Place a small drop of glue on the tip of the nail (fig. 1).
   b. Spread the glue evenly from the center to the sides.
   c. Let dry for about two minutes (without blowing, to avoid moisture).
   d. Using the very fine nail file, roughen the part coated with glue, then remove dust with the brush.
3. a. Repeat instructions 2a. and 2b.
   b. Dip the nail in baking soda before the glue dries (fig. 2) allowing the powder to adhere to the nail ; it dries instantly.
   c. using a brush, remove excess baking soda from the nail and the finger (fig. 3).
4. Repeat instructions 2a., 2b., and 2c.
5. Shape the nail with the file.
6. Polish the surface and tip of the nail.
7. Lacquer the nail.

For greater thickness, simply repeat this process as many times as needed.

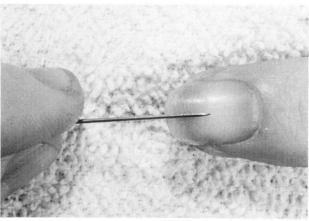

fig. 1

fig. 2

fig. 3

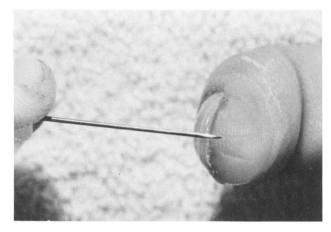

fig. 4

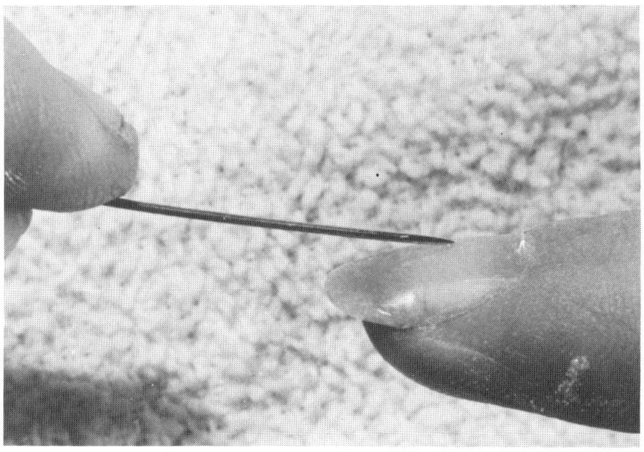

fig. 5

MAINTENANCE

- If the protective coating begins to come off due to wear, natural nail growth, or excess moisture, wait for it to dry before resetting it with glue, otherwise make a new protective coating.
- If the tip of the nail coating becomes detached from the nail, place a small drop of glue on along the tip of the nail using a pin (fig. 4).
- Ensure that the protective coating and the tip of the nail are always smooth to avoid catching them on the strings. Ensure also that the coating does not break, as it could tear off part of the natural nail.
- As the nail grows, add additional layers of protective coating and keep it at the desired length (fig. 5).
- To remove the nail coating, dissolve part of it using solvent, then file it down carefully, making sure not to inhale the dust from filing.

PRECAUTIONS

- Never cover the entire surface of the nail, only the first third or half, starting from the tip, in order to allow the root to breathe and grow.
- Avoid getting glue under the nail. If that happens, remove it.
- Never remove the protective coating by force because it could take with it precious layers of natural nail.
- Handle all the products with great care, especially the glue (avoiding contact with the eyes).
- Avoid border crossings when carrying baking soda in luggage...

Note : This process is effective, but it should be used in moderation (such as for nails broken at the last minute), because the cyanide contained in this type of glue ultimately damages the nail. Above all, nails require natural care. Vitamins (E) and trace-elements such as calcium and silicium, help to fortify them. Like hair, nails get stronger if they are clipped regularly (keeping a minimum length for playing).

BARS, PARTIAL BARS *(see FINGERINGS)*

The choice of a *bar* or *partial bar* is based on several closely related factors :

- the succession of fingerings into which it is to be inserted,
- the physical and mechanical availability of the hand,
- the interpretive goal (such as bringing out certain resonances).

The choice between a complete and a partial bar, on the one hand, and a fingering that requires the use of several fingers (which is theoretically less practical), on the other hand, is not an easy one. There are instances where the bar, when strummed, causes unwanted resonance in certain strings (*the unwanted effect of hammering* ; *see SLURS*). On the other hand, in the case where the bending of one of the fingers on the highest string(s) produces a more difficult and less rational fingering, the bar is the logical choice, even if it is only useful for one string.

In the pieces following this glossary, partial bars are indicated by the sign (b), occasionally followed by the fingering. When the sign is placed before the fingering, the finger, after having been used normally to produce the note on the string, is to be placed in the bar position without leaving the fret board, and simply by bending the knuckles :

a) bar position
b) partial bar position
c) normal fingering
d) knuckle bending, in the partial bar position

e) warming-up exercices for the knuckles of the left hand fingers

When more than four strings are involved, the bar is complete. This is notated using the sign C (*abbreviation for the Spanish word « cerra », meaning « bar »*). This sign is followed by a numeral designating the barred fret, and by a horizontal line indicating the length of the bar ; it is placed above the tablature.

CAPO

The capo is an accessory that is attached to the neck of the guitar, at the top of any fret. It acts as a movable nut, making it possible to change key by stopping all six strings at once.

The capo changes the relationship between interval and string tensions, bringing into play the shorter frets and reducing the distance between the strings and the fret board. Playing is thus made easier.

The modified string tension has an effect on intonation. Therefore, care must be taken to ensure that each string lies in a perfectly straight line when a capo is used (*see STRINGS, paragraph on tuning*).

The capo is not an integral part of the instrument, and therefore its use is a delicate matter. It should not be used systematically by the player who encounters difficulty, but rather to bring out certain tone colors, while maintaining the appropriate fingerings, or to adapt to a singer's vocal range.

The pieces in this book that are to be played with a capo are written directly in the key obtained using the capo.

CARING FOR THE GUITAR

(Conversation with George LOWDEN)

G.L. ; *For maintenance, I recommend that a good instrument should have a sturdy case, and that the guitar should not be able to move inside the case. The guitar should not be allowed to stay near a heat source, stored in direct sunlight, nor allowed to be in a car in warm weather. Excesses of dryness should be avoided by keeping a few plants in the room where the guitar is normally stored. If any damage appears on the guitar, it should be repaired immediately, as time will not help a damaged guitar's condition. In particular, for my guitars, I recommend that the satin finish be maintained by using a nonsilicone-type polish, which is not for gloss-finished furniture.*

P.B. : *Is it a good idea for guitarists to attempt their own repairs ?*

G.L. : *Generally, it is not a good idea, unless they have a good book on the subject of guitar repair, and are confident to be able to carry out the work. Truss rod adjustment should always be carried out by an experienced repairman, as should crack repairs or any internal work.*

FINGERINGS

This term is employed particularly for the use of the fingers of the left hand on the neck.

The more familiar the player becomes with the location of the notes, the more logically the fingers and hand deal with their horizontal and vertical movements, finding solutions for difficult passages more naturally. Nevertheless, this does not occur by itself, and it is up to the player to continue to develop his own capabilities. What is important is to leave oneself more open to more possibilities to choose the best fingering understand, after some time and with practice, that it is more appropriate in order to achieve that effect (*see TEMPO - MOVEMENT*).

Several factors contribute to the logic and fluidity of the fingers :

● a comfortable body position, nimble articulations, and relaxed muscles (*see HAND and BODY POSITION*).

● flexible and rational movement of the fingers :
  - they should remain as close as possible to the fret board and be relaxed, ready to *act* when and where needed, anticipating the position for each new fingering.
  - they should be rounded in order not to cut off the resonance of the other strings by grazing them inadvertently.
  - their efforts should be spacious and economical.
  - nails should be trimmed close in order to take advantage of the entire fleshy surface of the fingers.

● distributing the effort in the hand by placing the thumb under the neck for support ; this balances the opposing pressure and impulse of the other fingers. At times, it can even be taken off the neck, not counterbalancing the pressure of the fingers on the fret board.

Due to the width of the neck on classical guitars, the thumb is rarely used in fingerings on the fret board. On steel string guitars, where the neck is thinner, the thumb is often used to finger the bass strings. The hand and wrist are therefore more mobile around the neck. The palm, most often in contact with the neck, lends itself more to *chorus* vibrato effects (*see VIBRATO*). Nevertheless, this does not mean that any one type of fingering is for use only with certain types of instruments, for as guitar pieces evolve, so do techniques.

● Unwanted noise between finger changes should be kept to a minimum. Accuracy will be all the greater as the fingers are lifted the strings rather than slid (unless another effect is desired).

The sign  indicates that the resonance on all strings is to be stopped immediately by placing the left hand over the fret board, whether gently or strongly, and in all cases, producing a sound that becomes a voluntary rhythmic effect.

It is more desirable to cut off resonance at frets where harmonics may be produced (*see NATURAL HARMONICS and OPEN STRINGS*).

Changes in the left hand on the fret board are reminiscent of a cat slinking across a cluttered table without overturning a single object. At every step, it will choose the best spot to place its paws.

Thus, it is important that the player remain curious and not limit himself to what the fingers are familiar with or feel like doing at a given moment. Whatever the music, any new approach to fingerings is beneficial.

Note : The fingering of pieces in this book is indicated below the tablature or right next to the figure to which it corresponds (*see ATTACKS*).

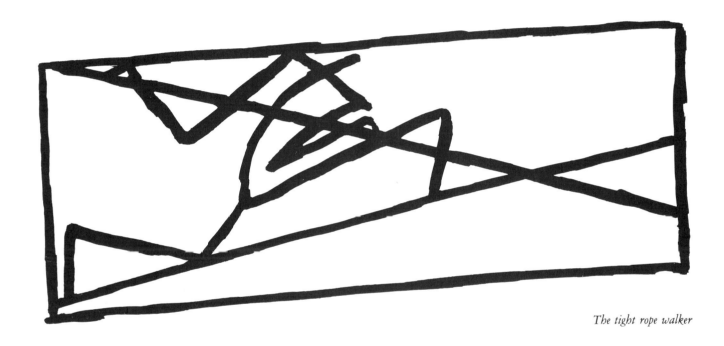

The tight rope walker

GLISSANDO

When two numerals or notes are connected by the sign ⌒ or ⌒ , the same finger is to slide along the neck from one note to the other. If a second finger is to take over from the first, the left hand fingering indicates that.

This work contains *glissandi* where the starting note is written (*see SLURS, ORNAMENTS*) either as *glissandi*, or rapid, discreet *portandi* whose starting note, left up to the interpreter's choice, is not mentioned in the score.

The beauty of the glissando effect stems from the sonorous balance created successively by the impulse of the right hand and the corresponding relay given by the left hand. It could almost be said to be a question of « looking out carefully », auditively. If the effect necessitates execution in two stages, the dynamic obtained must give the impression of a single gesture. This effect is not to be overused (*see VIBRATO, ATTACKS, and FINGERINGS*).

GUITAR MAKING

(Conversation with George LOWDEN).

P.B. : *Are there any trade secrets? Can you give us a broad outline of the construction of a Lowden without giving your secrets away?*

G.L. : *I don't suppose there are any real secrets as such in guitar building. However, putting into words exactly how I go about designing and building guitars is limited by the nature of the art of guitar building itself. I don't think that guitar building is primarily a science. I cannot go into my reasons for making this statement in this short space, but I have given the whole matter a lot of thought and there is no doubt that all three areas have a definite part to play.*

I have always tried to approach the question of guitar soundboard design from the point of view : « How can I get the soundboard to vibrate as evenly as possible over its whole surface? » Theoretically, it is impossible to make a guitar soundboard vibrate "evenly", because the soundboard, by its nature and shape and situation, will have areas of maximum and also minimum excursion. By the placing of braces into the surface of the guitar top, you are in fact disciplining these excursions or vibrations. However, the exact way in which this disciplining is done is one of the crucial factors in producing a guitar with even balance and good sustain and volume. The construction and design of the rest of the guitar plays an important part in the eventual tone of each guitar. The thickness of the back wood, the size and shape and depth of the soundbox, the construction of the neck and neck joint, the internal workmanship, etc., all these have a part to play in the quality of the guitar.

George Lowden

GLOSSARY OF ITALIAN EXPRESSIONS USED IN THIS BOOK

INDICATIONS OF VOLUME

- **pp** (pianissimo) — *very soft*
- **p** (piano) — *soft*
- **mp** (mezzo piano) — *moderately soft*
- **mf** (mezzo forte) — *moderately loud*
- **f** (forte) — *loud*
- **ff** (fortissimo) — *very loud*
- **sf** (sforzando) — *accented note or chord*

CHANGES IN VOLUME

- cresc. (crescendo) — *growing louder*
- dim. or dimin. (diminuendo) — *growing softer*

TEMPO INDICATIONS

- Largo — *broad*
- Larghetto — *not as broad as "largo"*
- Lento — *slow*
- Adagio — *slow, but faster than "lento"*
- Andante — *not fast, feeling of "walking"*
- Moderato — *moderate*
- Allegro — *brisk*
- Presto — *fast*
- Prestissimo — *very fast*
- accel. (accelerando) — *growing faster*
- rall. (rallentando) — *growing slower*
- tempo — *return to original tempo (after indicated tempo change)*
- senza tempo — *no set tempo*
- a piacere — *at the interpreter's pleasure : not rigorous, but remaining within the tempo*

OTHER EXPRESSIONS (in alphabetical order)

ad lib. (ad libitum) — *left up to the interpreter, who can accept or refuse to follow the notated indication, or improvise variations or embellishments.*

- al — *to*
- al fine — *to the end*
- al segno — *to the sign*
- aereo — *airy*
- affettuoso — *affectionate*
- affrettando — *becoming faster, as if excited*
- allegrezza — *cheerful*
- all'unisono — *in unison*
- animando — *growing animated*
- animato — *animated*
- appassionato — *passionate*
- assolato — *sunny*
- calmo — *calm*
- cantabile — *in a singing manner (melodious, flowing)*
- chitarra — *guitar*
- ciclico — *cyclical*
- confidenziale — *confidential*
- con — *with*
- con brio — *lively*
- con calore — *warmly*

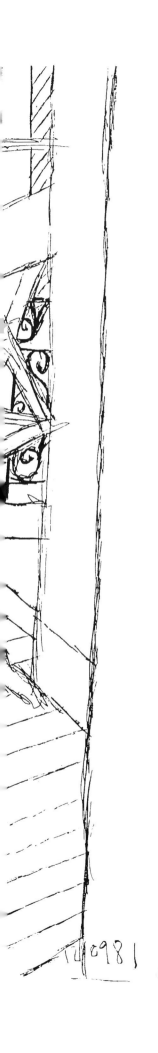

con moto	– *with movement (spiritedly)*
con sospeso	– *with suspense*
con spirito	– *with spirit*
con tenerezza	– *tenderly*
con umorismo	– *with humor*
D.C. (da capo)	– *return to the beginning*
danzante	– *in a dancing manner*
dolce	– *sweet*
dolcissimo	– *very sweet*
e-ed	– *and*
espressione	– *expression*
espressivo	– *expressive*
far girare	– *turn*
fermare	– *stop*
fine	– *(the) end*
generoso	– *generous*
giocoso	– *playful*
grazioso	– *gracious*
infeltrito	– *muffled*
inquietante	– *troubled*
legato	– *smooth, slurred*
legatissimo	– *very smooth, slurred*
legg. (leggiero)	– *light*
ma	– *but*
maestoso	– *majestic*
ma non troppo	– *not too (much)*
malinconico	– *melancholic*
marcato	– *strongly accented*
mesto	– *sad, pensive*
misterioso	– *mysterious*
morendo	– *dying away*
ottimista	– *optimistic*
pesante	– *heavy*
più	– *more (increasingly)*
più avanti	– *further*
poco	– *(a) little*
poco a poco	– *little by little*
refrain	– *refrain*
rinforz. (rinforzando)	– *with a sudden increase in force*
risoluto	– *resolutely*
ritard. (ritardando)	– *with a gradual slackening in tempo*
riten. (ritenuto)	– *restrained*
rub. (rubato)	– *fluctuation of speed within a phrase or measure, especially against a rhythmically stable accompaniment*
semplice	– *simple*
sempre	– *always*
sensuale	– *sensual*
sereno	– *serene*
soffocare le corde basse	– *damp the bass strings*
stacc. (staccato)	– *detached*
strofa	– *couplet*
strumentale (strum.)	– *instrumental*
sub. (subito)	– *suddenly*
tenuto	– *held for full note value*
tranquillo	– *tranquil*
variante	– *varying*
vigoroso	– *vigorous*
vocale	– *vocal*
voce	– *voice*
volta (pl. volte)	– *time (one, two times ; first, second time, etc.)*

HANDS AND BODY POSITION

On the one hand, each person has a particular anatomical configuration : more or less big hands ; broad palms ; long, spread out fingers ; etc. On the other hand there is the influence each of us can have over his anatomical make-up. The younger the person, the more flexible and malleable are his hands. The hands can be developed *to specifications*, as it were, to the logical extent that technique calls for it. This does not imply that it is necessary to begin from the cradle, nor that it is ever too late to train the hand. Some guitarists feel restricted and become discouraged, while progressive limbering-up exercises would help build up their confidence above and beyond any difficulties. Those difficulties can be surmounted thanks to an effective and rational work method, as well as a dose of patience.

The guitarist's hands must be flexible, strong, sensitive, and muscular (although that is not what makes the guitarist into a musician). The purpose of in-depth technique is not to break endurance and performance records, but rather to render oneself totally available to convey musical expression.

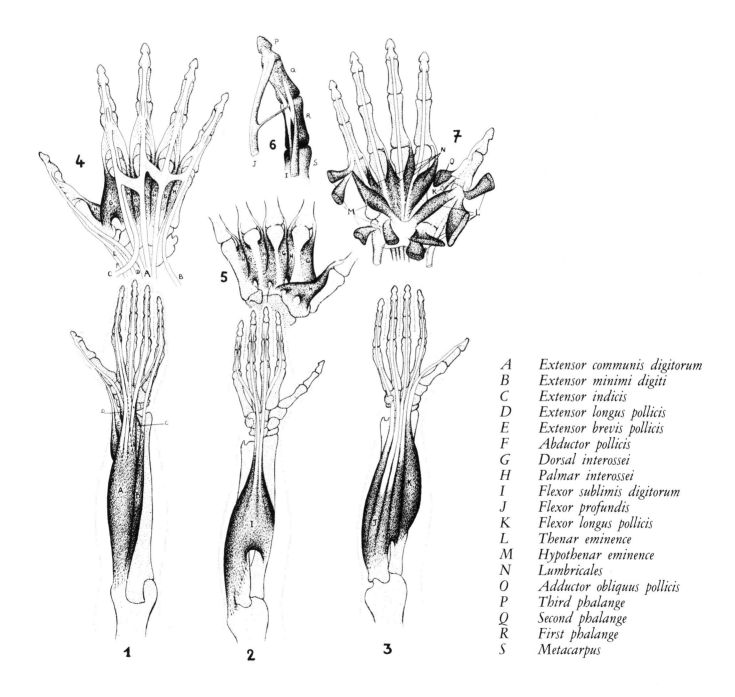

A	*Extensor communis digitorum*
B	*Extensor minimi digiti*
C	*Extensor indicis*
D	*Extensor longus pollicis*
E	*Extensor brevis pollicis*
F	*Abductor pollicis*
G	*Dorsal interossei*
H	*Palmar interossei*
I	*Flexor sublimis digitorum*
J	*Flexor profundis*
K	*Flexor longus pollicis*
L	*Thenar eminence*
M	*Hypothenar eminence*
N	*Lumbricales*
O	*Adductor obliquus pollicis*
P	*Third phalange*
Q	*Second phalange*
R	*First phalange*
S	*Metacarpus*

Note : Only those muscles of the right hand that are used in finger movements are shown.

The thumb, muscularly independent, contains three muscles : the extensor longus pollicis (D), the extensor brevis pollicis (E), and the abductor pollicis (F), which provide for extension (fig. 1). Contraction is carried out by the flexor longus pollicis (K, fig. 3), the adductor obliquus pollicis (O), and the thenar eminence (L, fig. 7).

Spreading apart and bringing together the fingers is made possible by the dorsal interossei (G) and the palmar interossei (H) (fig. 4 and 5), respectively.

The lambricales (N, fig. 7), flex the fingers tautened on the metacarpi. The lambricales of the index is the muscle used in producing barred chords.

On the posterior side (fig. 1), the extensor communis digitorum (A) is a muscle common to the four fingers. The index has its own extensor (extensor indicis, C), as does the little finger (extensor minimi digiti, B), which gives each of them greater freedom of movement than the middle or ring fingers.

On the anterior side (fig. 2 and 3), the flexor sublimis digitorum (I) bends the second phalange (Q) over the first phalange (R, fig. 6). The flexor profundis (J, fig. 3) bends the third phalange (P) over the second phalange (Q, fig. 6), and working together with the flexor sublimis digitorum (I), enables the fingers to bend over themselves.

The entire mechanism is lubricated by synovia.

warming-up exercices for both hands

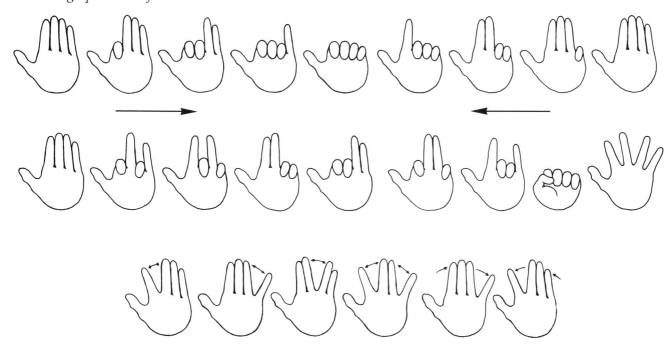

in order to dissociate the muscles composing the Flexor Profundis

Fingers and palms in contact, hands spread as much as possible.

The fingers exert pressure against each other while the palms come apart. The articulations of the elbows are horizontal, in the same axis as the pressure exerted by the fingers.

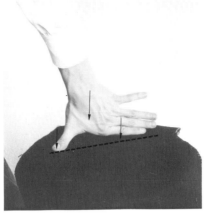

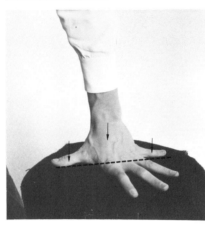

The muscles and tendons do not always work under pressure. There are alternating periods of relaxation, along the same lines as breathing : inhalation, exhalation.

There is a host of short exercises each of us can develop, for example, drumming the fingers of both hands on any surface, simultaneously and in a dissociated fashion, in different rhythms ; typing letters on a typewriter, etc.

The work carried out by the hands is also conditioned by the general attitude of the body. Generally speaking, holding the guitar requires a position that is twisted, curved, and asymmetrical, yet that position can be made as rational, comfortable, and harmonious as possible.

Note : We will not discuss here the classical manner of holding a nylon string guitar, even though many guitarists have played the classical guitar and have chosen to adopt a similar position when playing other types of guitars *(e.g. : Ralph TOWNER).*

The spine which is stable and remains properly in-line, even if the back is curved, enables the arms and legs to remain nimble, without feeling awkward. In this way, the muscles will not be contracted needlessly.

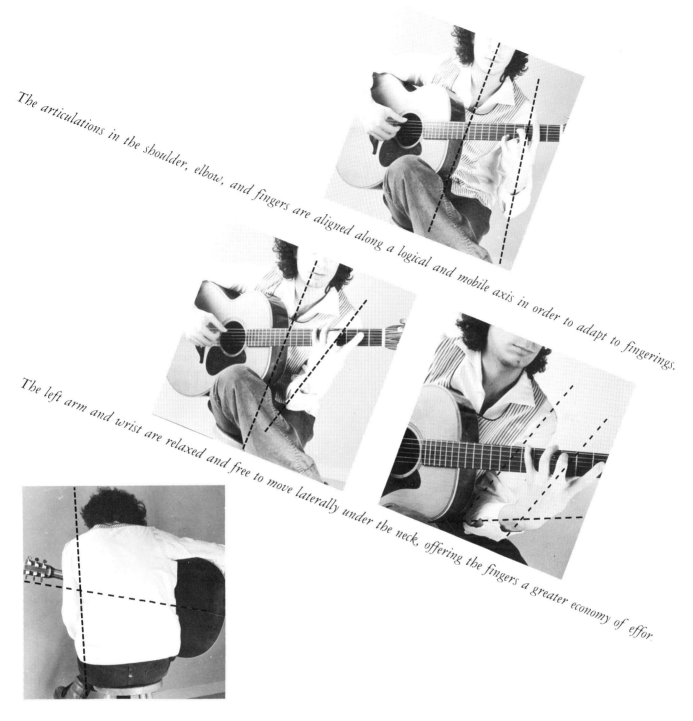

The articulations in the shoulder, elbow, and fingers are aligned along a logical and mobile axis in order to adapt to fingerings.

The left arm and wrist are relaxed and free to move laterally under the neck, offering the fingers a greater economy of effort.

The body of the guitar is in contact with the torso. The axis of the spine is practically perpendicular to that of the instrument. This example can be used as a guide for the player who has not yet found his own body position and manner of holding the instrument.

● As opposed to the classical position, where the guitar is chocked against the left thigh which is raised by having the foot rest on a footrest, balance can be also achieved by raising the right thigh, on which the instrument is resting.

● The rib cage is freed, even if the body "envelops" the guitar. The ribs, opening from the back, make it possible to breath by freeing the air column, even in what appears to be a closed position.

● The guitarist often uses his eyes. Thus, it is necessary to focus on objects in the distance without trying to look at the guitar table by rocking the guitar. By doing so, the player becomes dependent upon his sight, decreases his powers of concentration, and develops unnatural and uncomfortable positions. It is mostly thanks to virtual landmarks and habits picked up by the hands that fingerings fall into place.

The technique that develops, little by little, is not to be found only in the tips of the fingers ; it follows from a vaster physical logic which concerns the musician's entire corporeal attitude.

HARP EFFECT

The *harp effect* refers to an arpeggiated fingering. It consists in distributing, as much as possible, the notes of a melody over the different strings, and **holding** the successive fingerings in order to prolong the resonance of each of the strings. The ideal situation is to find a harmonious balance in the choice of fretted notes and open strings, to use well the *liaison* in fretted fingerings, in order to make them *flow* even more. (*see ARPEGGIOS, SLURS, FINGERINGS, OPEN STRINGS*).

While certain fingerings are painful for the hand, due to their stretch, the pain can be overcome by practicing the fingerings in order to limber up, adapt, and relax the muscles, tendons, and articulations (*see HANDS*). If difficulty persists, the fingers can *jump* from one note to the other, while maintaining the effect of a melody that is « plucked apart », in cascades of slurred notes.

In many instances, the left hand is used on the neck, and its alternately ascending and descending movement is logical and fluid. Once that has been learned, it is executed in a single gesture that is coordinated with the right hand, whose action is « geared down ». The fingers, passing from one string to the next, are more mobile and rapid (*see ATTACKS*), while the left hand, even at speed, is more economical in its movement along the fret board.

The logic of these fingerings helps the player acquire the needed ease and agility more quickly, even during fast passages. This creates *hammering* and polyphony through resonances, in the manner of harps and keyboard instruments (*see exercises, pgs. 63 and 122*).

INTERPRETATION

This term refers to indications in the score and to the personal initiative of the musician.

By means of conventional terms and symbols *(see MUSICAL NOTATION and GLOSSARY)* the composer tries to guide the interpreter towards the fulfilment of a precise intention. At times, the spirit in which music must be played can be seized readily (and almost without alternative) : the intention is neither indicated nor added on, but rather inherent in the composition. However, while respecting that intention, the player is free to take certain liberties (including breathing, rests, rubato, and vibrato). He depends on his condition, the given moment, and the listener, among other factors. It can be said that there are as many variables in interpretation as the number of times a given composition is played. (Reference is made here to actors and dancers). In order to give music a new complexion, the interpreter may choose a « path » that differs from the initial spirit, provided he does not do so systematically just to assert his own personality.

« The interpreter must possess an internal computer that ensures a balance between his two contrasting natures : the first dreams only of freedom and therefore rejects all restraint, but is nevertheless stopped by the second which knows how to keep a cool head ».

Mstislav ROSTROPOVICH

In spoken language, there are several possible inflections for any given phrase, although only one of them actually corresponds to the deep meaning of the thought expressed. The same holds true for the inflection of musical phrases. Moreover, if inflection requires a constant effort, the music will take life and live through the musician by means of *transparent* learned technique. Its purpose is not to demonstrate virtuosity nor a superficial esthetic form. In the *attic* of the memory, every individual grows roots, emotions, auditive (and other) memories, marks left by taste (or lack thereof). All those stored away « reserves », of which we sometimes cannot even guess their content or influence, make up a melting pot for our inspiration, a filter through which it passes, reconstitutes itself, and manifests itself at certain special moments, as new and original.

« What counts most for the guitarist is the vital "élan", those special moments when the life of a person passes through his guitar and gives him an inimitable accent, which can sometimes be expressed as a simple, different accentuation of a phrase, by a new phrasing, or, with some luck, by a totally original variation. Creation arises through playing. It is the emanation of the body of the musician, his psyche, his energy, the particular circumstances of the moment. Even technique and theoretical background must be the extension of the personality of every individual ».

Paco DE LUCIA

MUSICAL NOTATION (written with the invaluable assistance of Gérard REBOURS)

TABLATURE

Tablature is a system dating from the 14th century which goes hand in hand with an oral tradition that developed in Western Europe. The oldest of these known to this day was written for the organ in 1320. The word itself dates from the 15th century, and the system comprises letters, numerals, and various symbols. It was used essentially for solo instruments such as the organ, lute, guitar, harp, viola da gamba, and flute.

Certain plucked instruments had a string arrangement which rendered solfeggio notation difficult if not impossible. Thus, many technical details related to fingering and playing the instrument could only be notated using a tablature. The development of art music in Europe gave rise to new requirements with respect to musical notation which produced a breach between users of tablature and users of solfeggio. Those who used solfeggio notation criticized those who used tablature of employing a limited system by approaching music by means of notated fingerings to the detriment of harmonic coloring and interpretation.

While tablature flourished during the 16th and 17th centuries, particularly among lutanists, its disappearance from Europe towards the end of the 18th century was only logical. It reappeared early in the 20th century in the United States, where the development of oral tradition, due to the uprooting and immigration of ethnic groups, created a need for a musical notation that was practical and easily accessible. Towards 1960, thanks to the American *folk* movement, that system of notation was reintroduced in Europe, especially for the steel-string acoustic guitar.

The six lines, arranged horizontally, represent the six strings of the guitar, from the bass to the treble. The numeral 0 indicates that a particular string is to be played open. The other numerals indicate the fret on the fret board, counting from the nut to the soundhole.

Left hand fingerings are notated using small letters placed under or inside the staff next to the numerals to which they correspond *(see FINGERINGS and ATTACKS)*.

With the exception of measure bars, rhythm is not indicated in tablature since it appears in the solfeggio staff.

SOLFEGGIO

Solfeggio is a system of notation that dates from the time of the Greeks. The current system began to be developed in the 11th century. As opposed to tablature, which is *mute*, solfeggio directly designates notes and their value.

It would be too long to summarize the principles of musical notation here. For more complete information, consult appropriate works.

The same small letters, placed next to the notes, indicate the fingering of the right hand if needed *(see ATTACKS)*.

All indications concerning movement, nuances, and interpretation are written here in Italian (according to international musical convention, *see GLOSSARY*).

Lastly, for reasons of readability, the tablature occasionally contains signs that are used in solfeggio, and vice versa.

The sign ♩♩♩ , placed at the beginning of a piece, indicates that quarter notes are to be played in *triplet* time, giving the eighth notes a *swing* effect.

Note : Guitar music is written in and played from the treble clef. Once there was a transition between tablature and solfeggio, the guitar was written in the *tenor* clef, meaning that the notes sound an octave lower than written. For that reason, a small "8" should always appear under the clef to indicate that it sounds one octave below written pitch.

The richness and complexity of the guitar are enhanced by means of the multiple choice of fingerings and colors. We have preferred to use both notational systems simultaneously in this book, each of which reveals a different and yet complementary aspect of guitar music.

NATURAL HARMONICS

« Harmonics sound well on the guitar, and are used to advantage on many occasions ».
Hector BERLIOZ

DIRECT HARMONICS *(see exercice p. 98)*

The sound of a string vibrating independently over its entire length is the deepest it can produce. It is invariable, and is therefore called the *fundamental*. According to the physical principles of the vibration of strings, the fundamental creates other higher notes. This is the basis of the entire acoustical and harmonic system in music.

The different *harmonic sounds* are obtained by multiplying the vibrations of the *fundamental* at specific locations above the frets. The vibrating string grazed by the finger then divides itself, over its entire length, into from two to eight regular intervals.

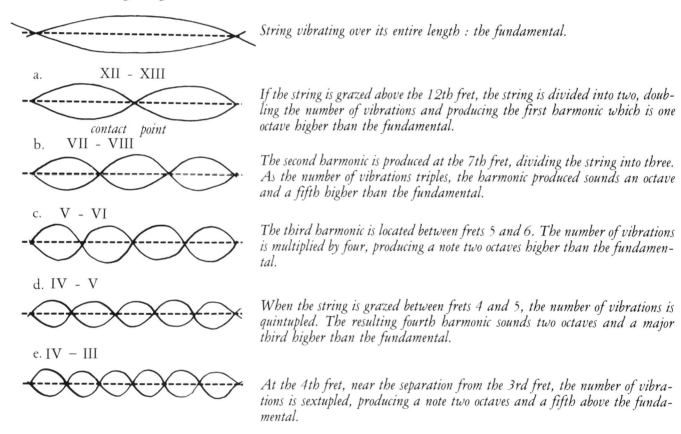

String vibrating over its entire length : the fundamental.

If the string is grazed above the 12th fret, the string is divided into two, doubling the number of vibrations and producing the first harmonic which is one octave higher than the fundamental.

The second harmonic is produced at the 7th fret, dividing the string into three. As the number of vibrations triples, the harmonic produced sounds an octave and a fifth higher than the fundamental.

The third harmonic is located between frets 5 and 6. The number of vibrations is multiplied by four, producing a note two octaves higher than the fundamental.

When the string is grazed between frets 4 and 5, the number of vibrations is quintupled. The resulting fourth harmonic sounds two octaves and a major third higher than the fundamental.

At the 4th fret, near the separation from the 3rd fret, the number of vibrations is sextupled, producing a note two octaves and a fifth above the fundamental.

The first five harmonics obtained naturally occur at intervals of an octave, octave + fifth, double octave, double octave + major third, and double octave + fifth higher than the fundamental :

(using the D-string for this example)

This principle can be applied to all the strings. For practice, look for the natural harmonics on each string and work on their sound for accuracy, length, and tone color *(see ATTACKS)*. Combine them, string by string, looking for varied combinations from one string to the next.

It is necessary to feel that the right hand is causing the vibration and that the left hand, once it has begun to feel the vibration in the flesh of the finger, produces the sound and removes itself from the string immediately afterwards.

The resonance of harmonics is prolonged for as long as the string vibrates. In addition, where time value is not specified in the pieces that follow, the intention is to prolong their resonance as long as possible by mixing them in with the notes that follow *(see OPEN STRINGS)*.

Note : Harmonics can be produced more easily by attacking the string near the bridge.

INDIRECT HARMONICS

The acoustic principle of harmonics is the same for all vibrating strings, regardless of their tension, volume, or length. When one of the fingers on the left hand presses a string at any fret whatsoever, thus playing the role of nut, the player obtains the same system of intervals between harmonics with respect to the fundamental *(see DIRECT HARMONICS)*.

As the finger(s) of the left hand are mobilized (in a fingering on one or more strings), the right hand has the double role of attacking the string with the middle finger, ring finger, or little finger, and creating the point of contact for the harmonic using the index, or occasionally even the middle finger. For that type of fingering, the interval between the finger that attacks and the one that produces the harmonic remains the same. The position of the right hand is specific and the wrist also gets into position with flexibility.

notation : harmonic + name of the finger that plays it + fret + name of the finger that attacks.

ex. *(in D A D G A D)* :

By learning these fingerings, the player obtains greater horizontal familiarity with the neck, particularly towards the end of the fret board, above the soundhole, and as far down as the bridge, where the locations are closer together and more subtle than above the frets.

Thanks to indirect harmonics, the instrument's high range is enhanced. At this juncture, I am thinking about the ingenious Canadian guitarist Lenny BREAU who made brilliant use of the possiblities and wealth of harmonics.

Sprite that delights
Vibrating string
Music so light
Music that sings

Who is to credit
When it pleases
'Tis the spirit
The guitar releases

Be off, in flight
Silken voice
Heat, blinding light
Sing, Doa, rejoice

Free as the air
Your way understand
Faith in me, dare
To the tips of your hands

Gérard CORNU

OPEN STRINGS

The richness of the guitar's resonance gives reason to increase the balance and variety of timbres by combining the use of *fretted* notes and *open strings*. Within the guitar family, the (steel-string) acoustic guitar stands out by the use of open strings and their resonance. Their material and their tension make their sound last longer than when using nylon strings (*see STRINGS*). Unlike fretted notes, whose sound can be controlled and *treated* by the left hand, open strings can leave the player with a sense of powerlessness, faced with the desire to alter their tone, and awkwardness over the mastery of the power of their volume. Despite that, the few influences possible on open strings are rich in nuances and coloration :

● the « dose » and quality of the right hand attack (*see ATTACKS*).

● the possibility of creating natural or *chorus* vibrato effects at all times by pivoting the resonating chamber, which also has an effect on the neck, which itself is guided by the left hand. This motion, transmitted to the instrument, *upsets* the vibrations inside the resonating chamber and causes them to come out in waves (*see VIBRATO*).

● by mixing the sound of open strings with that of fretted strings (*see FINGERINGS*) :

- as a unison : the open note is enriched by the *treated* (fretted) note, and vice versa.

- harmonized together : the resonance of open strings, which lasts as long as possible, acts as a backdrop to the *treated* notes.

● by stopping their resonance appropriately with the right hand or an appropriate left hand fingering.

In certain fingering sequences the use of the open strings usually helps to handle delicate transitions and imparts greater ease to the phrasing.

In the pieces that follow, the value of the notes on the open strings is generally fictitious, because unless any other intention is indicated in the score, the guitarist must compensate for their prolonged resonance, by « dosing » their attack as he sees fit, or replacing them by fretted notes, etc.

PAUSES

The pause is a space between notes that makes it possible to prolong the memory of what the ear has just heard after the sound of the note has faded. It also prepares the ear for listening to the sounds about to be produced. It can be a moment of relaxation, breathing, and transition between two movements or a moment that suspends the music while keeping the listener's attention mobilized. The quality of the pause establishes an indispensable link between the player and the listener. It must be respected before, during, and after the music.

« *The secret lies in knowing how to listen* ».
Paco de LUCIA

Munir Bashir, from Irak, playing Ud

RUBATO

This is an Italian word that means *stolen*.

« ... designates a special means of rendering note values unequal in execution, particularly by prolonging the initial notes and rushing the final notes ».

Théorie Complète de la Musique, CHAILLEY et CHALLAN, éditions LEDUC, Paris.

« *I consider each day of my life as a gift from God, and I try to live it to the fullest, in a manner different from those days past. If you were to ask me how many hours a day I practice the cello, I would be unable to tell you. I can let it go for several days, and then, suddenly, seized by passion over a new work, for example, I will start to practice like a madman. Another strange thing I do is to avoid walking in Spring, while in Autumn I love to get back to nature. And I'm thrilled by those changes in mood that make every day different. You might call that "rubato"* ».

Mstislav ROSTROPOVICH

SHORT HISTORY OF THE GUITAR FAMILY

(with the assistance of Gérard REBOURS)

The ancestors of the guitar come from a vast geographical area and date back several thousand years.

The representation of a long-necked instrument with resonating chamber, held obliquely or almost horizontally, was found on a seal from Mesopotamia dating back to the 24th century B.C. Other representations are to be found on Babylonian bas-reliefs dating from the 9th century B.C. An instrument of the same type was found in the crypt of the Egyptian singer Har MOSE (1500 B.C.) and one very similar on a Hittite relief in Asia Minor (1300 B.C.). Their « figure eight » shape makes them relatives of the guitar (*tar* means *string* in Persian). Instruments of the same family also existed during Roman times.

A 9th century psaltery from Stuttgart, during the Carolingian era, is decorated with the figure of an instrument with a very elongated and narrow body which was found the following century, in 926, in the manuscript entitled *Commentarius Super Apocalyptus*, accompanied by others with pear-shaped bodies, played either with plectrum or bow.

Although some instruments used in Western art music may have disappeared or undergone incessant transformations throughout the years, others of more popular origin, from Africa, Asia, Eastern Europe, and more countries still, have remained practically identical to the oldest of the family.

Beginning in the 13th century, in the sculptures and illustrations of musical collections (such as the celebrated *Cantigas de Sancta Maria*, attributed to *Alfonso X El Sabio*), the figure-eight shape of the body, tightly incurved sidewalls, appeared regularly in one of a number of variants.

The lute, brought to Spain by the Maurs during the 10th century, continued to evolve before ultimately disappearing towards the end of the 18th century in the Germanic countries, contrary to many Mediterranean countries, where it remained in common use (for example, the classical Arabic lute). The lute is not an ancestor of the guitar. Although both are derived from instruments with elongated bodies, long strings and necks, they developed in parallel, in the same way as the viols, violins, mandolins, etc.

A painting dating from 1510 shows a viol greatly resembling the guitar, known as *vihuela de mano*, or *viola a mano* which was plucked with the fingers, unlike the others that were played *de arco* (with a bow). It was used in Spain and Italy. Larger than the guitar, it had six rows of double strings.

After 1600, the *baroque guitar* made its appearance. It was smaller and had five strings with the tuning A-D-G-B-E. This instrument, of subtle technique, was used for two centuries.

After having given rise to numerous variants, the six single-string guitar, with its present-day tuning, established itself at the beginning of the 19th century, The methods of instrument making and the size have changed since then. The electric guitar and steel-string acoustic guitar both came from the United States during the 20th century.

« (...) *The guitar, in fact, is a new instrument, which is not really tempered, and there are certainly a multitude of other guitars yet to be invented. The guitar is not the end of the line. It is a means, not an end. (...)* »

Egberto GISMONTI

Sculpture, Cathedral of St.-Jacques de Compostelle (Gallicia, Spain)

SINGING

The voice, like the guitar, is an instrument by means of which music comes alive. Closely related to the imaginary and to musical conception, it is an almost instantaneous means, also the most natural, of expressing inspiration, externalizing the music each of us hears inside himself, as if it were a subterranean spring. The moment the water becomes visible to the eye, at the earth's surface, is like the moment when the voice reaches the ear.

The voice is different from instruments in that its production requires no external device. Conception, exteriorization, and interpretation all originate in the same *place*. The voice is our first instrument, and it can be combined quite naturally with other instruments, even though it has always been extolled as a solo instrument of its own right. Aside from simple accompaniment, guitar and voice can blend in composition and improvisation. The colors of their timbres are mutually enriching. By *working* the voice, both alone and in combinations with other instruments, it is possible to enhance their melodic, rhythmic, and harmonic coordination.

Singing has a relaxing effect while playing. Moreover, breathing is a sort of *fuel*. Proper breathing releases unwanted tension, leaves the body available, and clears the soul. Music can flow all the more freely.

If the player sings, the natural agility he feels with his voice instills in him the desire to play his instrument with even greater lightness, to the point where the mechanical intermediary impedes expression as little as possible.

Luxor tradition : Ahmed Mohamed Barrayn (Egypt)

« I exercise constantly, I sing all the time. I try everything that comes to mind. I have no method for exercising, I just sing as often as I can. (...) When I teach, I always encourage my students to listen to no one for a certain amount of time, especially when they are trying to determine who they really are. The best way to find out who you are is to stand in front of a mirror and sing for yourself, to see what comes out ».

Bobby MC FERRIN

SLURS - ORNAMENTS

When two or more mumerals or notes are connected by the sign ⌣ or ⌒ , they are slurred. The right hand only plucks the string once although at least two consecutive notes are produced.

Note : Do not confuse this with the *tie* which connects two notes of the same pitch without calling for the repetition of the second note.

In an *ascending* direction (0⌒2) , the finger hammers on the string. Conversely, when *descending* (2⌒0) , the finger pulls off the string. These effects save the right hand a great deal of effort, as it is relayed by the left hand which *attacks*. This contributes to more fluid phrasing. Once the player has mastered fingerings, he can naturally turn to the subject of *ornamentation.*

Embellishments have been ubiquitous in the vocal and instrumental music of the peoples of Africa and the Far East for thousands of years. In Europe, they have been used to enrich melodies by extending the sound of the notes on instruments with short-lasting resonance (such as the harpsichord and the lute).

It would be too longwinded here to discuss all the types of embellishments, their origin, and the manifold possibilities of interpreting them. We will see how some of them are applied through the pieces in this book.

Ornements are notated separately, using small notes or symbols. They have no set time value *per se* ; they *borrow* time from the note they embellish.

In the *mordent*, indicated by the symbol ∿ or ⸕ placed over a note,

The number of notes played depends on the number of "zigzags" in the symbol :

and generally respect the key or mode of the piece in which they appear.
When an alteration is desired, it is indicated by a (♭) or (♯) placed over the symbol :

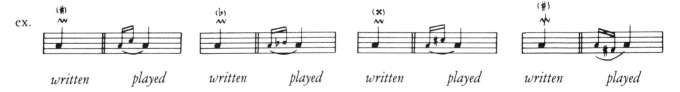

Note : Unless otherwise indicated, mordents are always slurred.

● *Grace notes*, written in small characters within the staff, have no set time value. They can be played very quickly, before the note they embellish, or be included in the time value of that note, in which case they are known as appogiaturas.

• *The trill*, another ornament, is indicated by the symbol  placed over the note. This is a rapid alternation between two notes, the equivalent of a long mordent (although the notes may or may not be slurred).

When executing these ornaments, it is important to use the right hand with respectively proportional energy and precision, both to the number of notes to be played, and to the quality of their sound. There is no need to "force" them, what is essential is to control the pressure of both hands : the right hand produces the note and the left hand *captures* and *shapes* it.

This is a case where *vibrato* is often used to color and unify (its acoustical principle is very close to the musical *drawing* of ornaments). *(See VIBRATO, ATTACKS)*.

STRINGS

(written with the assistance of Gérard REBOURS)

Earlier strings were made of animal gut. They could be simple (round, or braided for the lowest strings), sometimes dipped in a coloring liquid, probably to make them more sonorous or more resistant. It was only towards the mid-1900s that nylon strings — far more resistant but producing a flaccid tone — came into use. Gut strings, covered with a more or less tightened metal wire, were introduced around 1660. Steel strings were used on the *chitarrone* and the *chitarra battente*.

The work I have undertaken, which is illustrated in part in this book, essentially concerns the steel-string guitar. The choice of string quality and gauge, which determine their tension, is of the utmost importance. It should be possible to change from the standard tuning (E-A-D-G-B-E), where the neck is exposed to normal pressure, to open tunings, which alter the tension of certain strings. If the guitarist uses several different tunings, it is well to give preference first to a gauge that is adapted to open tunings while being as appropriate as possible for the standard tuning. This compromise gives priority to open tunings, because they respond to a greater number of needs : the mixture of gauges must rebalance the tension of the strings and guarantee maximum resonance.

Without giving more precise indications, it is advisable for all the strings to be flexible, and for their tension to be a compromise between *light* and *extra-light* gauges, while maintaining the possibility of using *medium* gauge for the strings that have to be tuned down. In this respect, it should be remembered that the thicker the strings the shorter their lifespan. *Heavy* and *medium* gauge should be avoided for the other strings, because they could damage instruments that have not been designed to withstand the added tension. Furthermore, the tactile sensation felt by both hands, which is improved by string flexibility, must be maintained. That sensation helps enrich the perception of nuances and tone colorations while conditioning the player's sensitivity to the instrument *(see ATTACKS and FINGERINGS)*.

Guitarists have therefore taken the initiative of putting together specific mixed sets of strings to meet all these needs, while awaiting their introduction on the market, or having them manufactured directly by a string maker.

1. - PUTTING ON THE STRINGS (for steel strings)

New strings are particularly sensitive to temperature changes. Generally speaking, they lose their tune for some time before stabilizing. It is possible to shorten that stabilization time by putting them on in the following manner (thanks to Bill KEITH for this information) :

The string is placed through the holes of the machine heads perpendicular to the neck. (a)

The string is knotted to keep it in place once and for all, after having wound it once around the machine head. (b)

When tying the knot, a certain additional length of string should be left free in order to wind it around the machine head a number of times. The machine head is then turned with a string winder, while keeping the string taut with the index finger of the other hand and by pressing on it with the middle finger to ensure that it is wound taut, tight, and as low as possible on the machine head. (c)

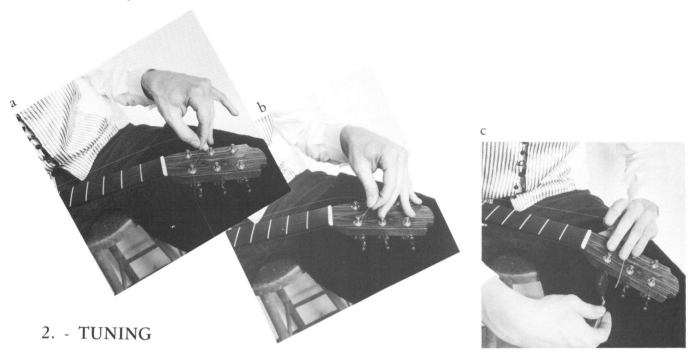

2. - TUNING

Once the strings are put on, tightened, and tuned, they are to be pulled by their middle, away from the guitar and perpendicular to the neck, firmly but with care *(see 1)*, or else by pressing on them over the soundhole *(see 2)*, or between the nut and the machine heads *(see 3)*. These procedures, repeated several times, speed up string stabilization by making them lose as much tension as possible.

Moreover, in order to keep strings from tightening or loosening rapidly, the machine heads should be turned to the very end of their screw thread. There should be no lost motion in the gearwheels. In order to help the strings slide smoothly, it is possible to coat the bottoms of the grooves of the nut with a soft lead pencil, especially those of the G and D strings (4th).

Once the strings are put on and tuned, additional lengths of string should be cut at the machine heads, because they can cause injury or unwanted noises.

The guitar's tuning should be checked regularly with a tuning fork, and each pair of strings should be checked for harmonic/open string unisons. While aiming for the *perfect* tuning, the ear is trained to hear sounds with greater accuracy *(see NATURAL HARMONICS).*

Tuning is precious and the time it takes is always justified compared to the discomfort one can feel – when listening to a guitar *out of tune*. Don't hurry or think that the audience might become impatient ; the performance begins with a careful, concentrated tuning of the guitar.

Note : New strings sometimes have defects. In order to verify their accuracy, play through the harmonics and compare them with the corresponding fretted sounds, using the 12th fret as a guide. If the two notes (separated by an octave) are not perfectly in tune, it is better to replace the string than to readjust the neck or the saddle and the nut. In addition, wear and oxidation tend to change the density of the strings and make them sound off key (check the 12th fret). If they cannot be tuned, they should be replaced.

3. - CARE *(see THUMB PICK)*

When strings are *broken in*, they can last quite a long time (depending on the acidity of the perspiration in the fingers), and their oxidation can be checked by cleaning them completely with a cotton cloth after playing. Worn strings are more *docile*, although their brilliance and power, particularly in bass notes, fade quickly.

TEMPO - MOVEMENT - METRONOME

The metronomic beat or tempo of a piece is indicated on every score, either by means of a numeral indicating the number of metronome beats per minute and usually preceded by the sign " ≃ " (meaning *approximately*), or else by Italian terms indicating the nature of the movement, such as *Largo or Allegro (see MUSICAL NOTATION, GLOSSARY OF ITALIAN TERMS).*

Metronomic beat is not indicated imperatively and is not meant to be taken as an exact indication. Very often, it indicates the maximum tempo above which the piece would lose its character. Thus, it is preferable to play more slowly than the tempo indicated rather than more quickly. Furthermore, on the subject of speed, one essential item should be stressed : the player must never feel rushed to get to the end of a piece. He should take his time to decipher and interpret it.

In other words, in order to arrive progressively at mastery of a movement, it should be played very slowly at first, with as much musicality as possible. This imparts self-assurance and stability. Contrary to the impatience the player often feels, this is the fastest method of learning a piece.

It is important to understand the difference between the terms *a piacere* (as the player wishes, without sticking strictly to meter) and *senza tempo* (no meter indicated).

The value of the notes is indicated and will serve as a guide. Interpretations should « breathe », with the understanding that the pause is a fundamental element in musical dynamics *(see PAUSES, and INTERPRETATION).*

The metronome, while not indispensable, could be of aid to those who need more assurance with their tempo. Above all, it helps support the evolution of the player's technique and his aptitude to master any beat. Once a phrase has been learned slowly, it can be sped up progressively while maintaining stability of execution achieved at the very outset, until the player brings the piece up to the tempo indicated. It is often preferable to play slower than one's capacity, exercising restraint.

THUMB PICK *(see ATTACKS)*

This accessory, made of tortoiseshell or plastic, is placed over the right thumb. It has been used for many string instruments for many centuries and in many countries. Today, it is used only rarely, and has almost disappeared from use in Europe. In some countries, the ancient technique of the thumb pick has remained well established alongside their traditional music (for example, the Chinese *pipa*).

In the United States, it has continued to be an integral part of the technique for playing the banjo, the dobro, the steel guitar, and the pedal-steel guitar, among others. The *picking* technique for guitar, was made popular by Merle TRAVIS, Doc WATSON, Chet ATKINS, Jerry REED and numerous others. One of the aspects of this technique is to reinforce and single out the sounds of the bass strings, which are alternated and damped, over which a melodic line is played. The pick is used mainly for playing on steel strings, rarely on nylon strings.

Its use requires that the thumb work and be located differently with respect to the strings. The thumb is parallel and the pick is perpendicular to the strings. The attack is drier than with the bare thumb (attacking the strings at an angle). By damping the bass notes, it is also natural for the little finger to rest on the table in order to support the hand. These techniques should only be used from time to time, and therefore not be applied systematically *(see ATTACKS)*.

The effects produced by using a thumb pick fit in with a need for a precise musical intention, whatever the style of music being interpreted. However, in the long run, the pick upsets the balance of the entire hand. It produces unwanted noises and reduces the range of possible tone colors. The bare thumb, on the contrary, which remains in direct contact with the string, offers greater control of touch, producing warmer, richer timbres. Thus, while the thumb pick offers the advantage of increased dynamics, it cuts down on tone colors. Moreover, the pick helps wear out the strings, causing them to lose their sharpness and brilliance more rapidly *(see STRINGS)*.

By practising both techniques, the player will notice (unless he has a very marked preference for one style) that the thumb pick should be used in specific instances. For those who think that the habit is too strongly ingrained, it is never too late to approach and improve the technique of the bare right hand.

VIBRATO

Vibrato is a light, more or less rapid variation of the pitch of a note sounding continuously. This variation can be as broad as a fourth, depending on the instrument.

In ornaments such as the *mordent* or *trill*, where there is an alternation between two notes, the interval between the notes is generally a half-step or a whole-step *(see SLURS-ORNAMENTS)*. Vibrato allows for finer intervals, such as the quarter-tone and the eighth-tone.

It enriches and prolongs notes, leaving the ear with the impression that the sound is continuing even when it has stopped.

There are many ways of causing the notes on the guitar to vibrate : both hands acting on the strings, on the neck, at various locations on the body.

Notes on the guitar are produced differently from those on the piano. The guitarist shapes and refines them somewhat, just as a painter blends his colors.

Here are some different techniques for producing vibrato :

● The finger, while pressing on the string, causes a more or less rapid vibration without leaving the axis, and by moving the finger in a direction parallel to the strings. The finger and the hand both remain perpendicular to the neck and the impulse for the effect comes from the elbow articulation.

This vibrato is generally used on nylon strings.

Vibration can develop slowly or rapidly, from the bass notes to the treble notes. It can move towards the treble notes, in which case, the movement of the finger comes closer to the top of the fret, or in the bass notes, where the finger lies closer to the bottom of the fret.

This is a nonvibrating sound :

vibrato moving upwards :

downwards :

in the treble and bass :

slow vibrato :

fast vibrato :

● The finger, while pressing down on the string, pulls it alternately upwards and downwards, bringing it back to its axis thus creating several waves. The deepest note is the original note. The impulse is given by the wrist and the hand remains perpendicular or oblique with respect to the neck. This vibrato is often used on electric or steel-string acoustic guitars.

- While the finger stays in the same fret, it is possible to shift from one note to a higher note : *ex.* C ↗ D♭, C ↗ D, C ↗ E, C ↗ F, using *stretched* vibrato (*portamento*, in Italian).

The variation in pitch is broader than when using simple vibrato. This effect corresponds to the *glissando* used on fretless plucked string instruments such as the *classical Arabic lute.* It is highly elaborate in Indian music (on the *sitar*), in Chinese music (on the *pipa*), and even in blues (on the electric or acoustic guitar), among others.

- The *chorus* vibrato (the name comes from the electroacoustic effect that accentuates the undulation of notes) is used mostly with steel-string instruments in which it enriches the open resonances, compensating for the occasional desire to exert some influence over their sound using the fingers (which cannot be done with fingerings). The left hand pushes and pulls the neck, forwards and backwards, while the right arm and torso act as counterweights against the body of the guitar. This gives the entire instrument a see-saw motion that prolongs and diffuses the resonances outside the soundhole in waves *(see OPEN STRINGS).*

- Another example of vibrato comes from guitarist Alberto PONCE : a very clear variation in the intensity of the sound through finger contact at precise points of the table (at the bottom, to the right of the bridge).

- There is yet another method which consists in pressing on the strings between the nut and the machine heads.

All these types of vibrato enhance the texture of the sound, adding sensuality. As they give guitar playing a special character, the player must pay particular attention not to alter the musical context with stylistic attributes, but rather use vibrato to « exalt » the music and not make it the music's *raison d'être.*

Vibrato is a reflection of emotion. Music touches us when the amplitude of vibration is *in sync* with those of movements that are familiar to the soul. In this book, that effect is not noted ; it is left up to the interpreter's good taste, as if it were a series of drawings to be colored in.

« *The vibration of the soul and the soul of the vibration meld in the guitar's body. Each note is an arrow of love* ».

Emilio PUJOL

PUMPKIN SOUP

A tip : In order to make the soup, it is necessary for the pumpkin to be in season. It is better to prepare the soup in advance as it is ever more delicious when reheated.

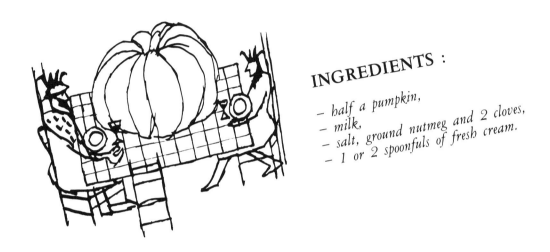

INGREDIENTS :
- half a pumpkin,
- milk,
- salt, ground nutmeg and 2 cloves,
- 1 or 2 spoonfuls of fresh cream.

Peel the pumpkin and cut into cubes. Put it in a pot and cover with milk.

Add salt, pepper, nutmeg, and cloves. Cook over a low flame, partly covered. Mix from time to time, to avoid the pumpkin from sticking.

After about one hour, check the consistance of the pumpkin. If cooked enough, remove from heat.

Half an hour before serving, remove cloves and puree the soup.

Before reheating, Tofu cut into small cubes can be added.

At the last minute, add 1 or 2 spoonfuls of fresh cream.

It's delicious, so invite Cinderella !

THE RETURN FROM FINGAL
(trad. Ireland ; adapt. : Pierre BENSUSAN)

DADGAD
(capo 3)

« Early Pierre Bensusan » (Lost Lake Arts, division of Windham Hill, Distribution : A & M)

à Jack Treese

© 1977, CÉZAME, 2 rue Flèchier, 75009 Paris, France

All rights reserved for all countries

ARPEGES

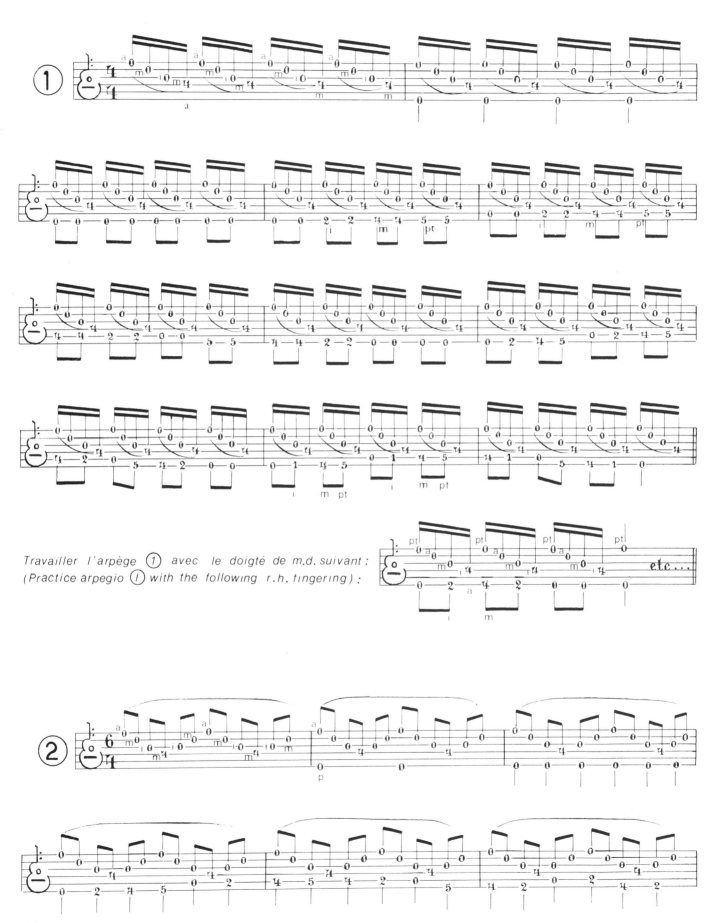

4 GRAIN BREAD

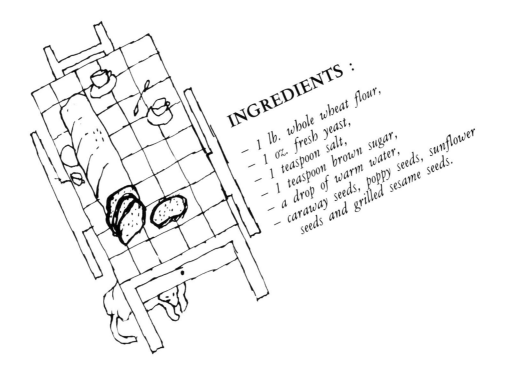

INGREDIENTS :
— 1 lb. whole wheat flour,
— 1 oz. fresh yeast,
— 1 teaspoon salt,
— 1 teaspoon brown sugar,
— a drop of warm water,
— caraway seeds, poppy seeds, sunflower seeds and grilled sesame seeds.

Preheat the oven for 15 mn (400-450°).

Make a well in the center of the flour, add crumbled yeast and a drop of warm water. Mix in more flour, cover and set aside for about 20 minutes.

Add the seeds and the rest of the warm water. Knead the bread, cover and set aside for another 40 minutes.

Form one or more loaves of bread, brush them with a little water or an egg yolk. Flour lightly, indent the surface of the bread with the tip of a knife.

Put the loaves in a cool place for a couple of minutes. Place in preheated oven and bake for 30 to 40 minutes (medium oven).

Keep an eye on the bread ; even if the crust of the bread is well formed, this does not necessarily mean that the bread is done.

The bread can be kept fresh in a dish-cloth for quite a while.

LE VOYAGE POUR L'IRLANDE
(Pierre BENSUSAN)

DADGAD

« Musiques » (Lost Lake Arts, division of Windham Hill, distribution : A & M)
« Compilations » (Chant du Monde, distribué par Harmonia Mundi)

à Serge Frochot

© 1979, CÉZAME, 2 rue Fléchier, 75009 Paris, France

All rights reserved for all countries

AMANI

Atanase oublié m'est revenu sans rides,
Son histoire filée par les mots de grand-mère,
Magicienne de l'âtre où dort le fou du feu.
Quand l'alchimie des fées remplaçaient nos chamailles,
Nous nous chauffions les mains contre nos bols de lait ;
Quand craquaient les parquets, ils corsaient les histoires.
Sur un fond de forêt, on dégustait la peur :
Le galop des chevaux nous courait sur la peau,
La colère de l'ogre nous attrapait au ventre,
Mort de soif Atanase, j'aurais cassé mon bol,
S'il marchait seul dans l'ombre, on était sous ses pas,
Et quand nos yeux buveurs de mensonges dorés
Découvraient un palais et la table de miel,
Une attente éblouie, le fondant des gâteaux et les yeux de la fée...
Amani se taisait, Atanase dormait,
Le soir nous avait pris à moitié dans ses bras,
Le feu nous rappelait qu'on était tout petit,
Mais que jamais le froid ne mangerait nos doigts.

Forgotten Athanase came back to my memory.
A tale of wizardry woven by Grand-mother's words :
Beside the dancing fire-fool, she would become skilled in magic.
When fairies' alchemy replaces tricks and games,
We could feel the soft warmth above our mugs of hot milk.
When floor boards creaked, it would add fear to our dream.
The sound of secret galloping would run on our skin,
The ogress in anger would leave us breathless,
And in the heart of unknown woods, every noise around
Would mingle thrill with our joy...
Had Athanase died of thirst, I would have dropped my cup,
If he were to walk in the dark, I would be under his footsteps.
And when our eyes, drinking these golden lies,
Discovered a castle as the last dazzling sight,
Athanase gathered honey from the eyes of a princess,
Then he would fall asleep and Amani fell silent...
The night had clasped us half-way in its arms,
The flames reminded us that here we were still kids,
But never would the cold come nipping at our fingers.

Doatea

THE RAKKISH PADDY

(trad. Ireland ; adapt : Pierre BENSUSAN)

DADGAD

à Pat Sheeran

« Musiques » (Lost Lake Arts, division of Windham Hill, distribution A & M)

Reel ♩ ≃ 86

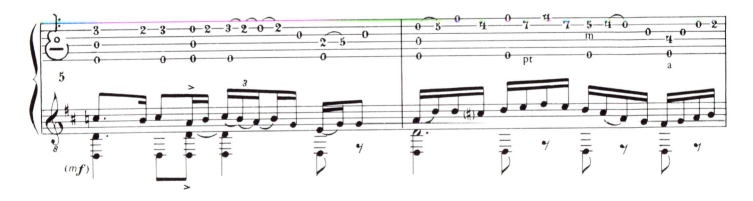

© 1979, CEZAME, 2 rue Flechier, 75009 Paris, France — All rights reserved for all countries

A garden
resembling a palace
with hawthorn and lilac tapestries
jasmine ceilings
iridescent shadows

You await me there, disguised as a sorceress
at the foot of the gallows swings a hanged man

I will meet you again, with an owl in my hair, a bullfrog in my throat, a dog on my heels. You will cast out the hanged man and strangle me with love. Wolf and she-wolf, seeking refuge from the snow, will want to devour you. The scent of your skin will entice them to death.

You
  Now
    Very lonely
      Chilled to the bone.

The smell of frost to make you forget that this was once a garden.

Francine Paillet.

PRÈS DE PARIS/REELS

(Pierre BENSUSAN/Trad. Ireland ; arrgt : Pierre BENSUSAN)

FGDGCF
(capo 4)

« Early Pierre Bensusan » (Lost Lake Arts, division of Windham Hill, distribution : A & M)

à Frédéric Leibovitz

© 1975, CÉZAME, 2 rue Fléchier, 75009 Paris, France

All rights reserved for all countries

FINE *The Morning Dew*

57

DE TRILPORT A FUBLAINES

(trad. arrgt : Pierre BENSUSAN/Pierre BENSUSAN)

DGDGCD
(capo 2)

« *Early Pierre Bensusan* » *(Lost Lake Arts, division of Windham Hill, distribution : A & M)*

à Josiane et Loïc Tréhin

© 1975, CÉZAME, 2 rue Fléchier, 75009 Paris, France

All rights reserved for all countries

DADGAD

L'EFFET HARPISANT

© 1985, Pierre BENSUSAN, P.O. Box 411, Mill Valley, CA. 94941. U.S.A.   All rights reserved for all countries

HEMAN DUBH

(trad. Scotland ; adapt : Pierre BENSUSAN)

DADGAD
(capo 3)

« Musiques » (Lost Lake Arts, division of Windham Hill, distribution : A & M)

à Alan Stivell

1979, CÉZAME, 2 rue Flèchier, 75009 Paris, France

All rights reserved for all countries

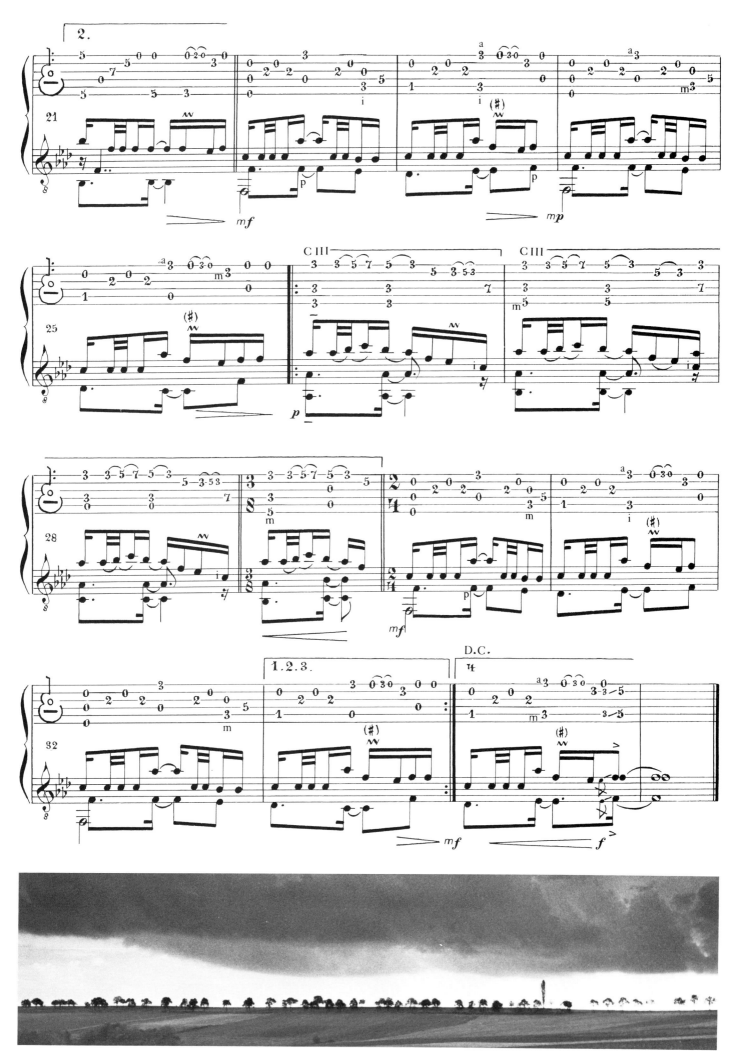

MAURICE AU PAYS DES MERVEILLES
(Maurice in Wonderland)
(Pierre BENSUSAN)

DADGAD

« Musiques » (Lost Lake Arts, division of Windham Hill, distribution : A & M)

FINE PARABOLE DE L'AMÈRE CONFITURE D'ORANGES

Amertume,
Confies-toi mon ange
Confit d'ange amer
Fais-moi don de confidences
Défies-toi des orages amers
Enfuis-toi en dormant
Tu dors ?... Dis, amant ?
Tu rêves ?
A quoi ?
Aux toitures, d'Eve,
De confit d'oie dorée - vie d'ange, conflit adoré -
Aux tuiles oranges, aux fils d'antan,
Aux toitures d'orge et aux anges là-haut qui filent.
Tu as froid ?
Couvres-toi, danses au son du sanfona
Et rendors-toi l'âme au chaud.
Oh... l'aile noire du cauchemar :
Les serres du condor étouffent le chant distillé de l'archange Cythère ;
Perché au bout de l'île en guerre, fait basculer l'oiseau de mer...
Ils n'avaient pas fini leur duel que les draps s'envolent en claquant,
Défaisant l'ourlet des paupières, te jetant au sol de ton lit.
Toits blancs au lever,
Tu ranges tes rêves, figé par leur audace amère...
Tu sens ? L'odeur sucrée en parallèle ?
Ta mère fait cuire la confiture de figues,
Coulant dans sa voix la légende :
« Comment les anges confondirent les tuiles oranges des toits
Et l'écorce des fruits d'or : ils firent une confiture de fées
En épluchant les tuiles du faîte. Ils écorchèrent leurs doigts de figues,
Les entourèrent de fils dorés.
Ils riaient fort, dénouant leur manteau de soie,
Espiègles plus que recueillis,
Faisant des jeux avec les mots et des signes loin des croix ;
Perchés sur les poutres à claire-voie,
Ils avaient l'air si amusés que la nef soit privée de toit :
« Les ors durent et les cons fondent... » ils disaient.
Soudain la foudre fendit l'arche et l'orage fondit sur eux.
Les anges affolés soupirèrent, se turent et confièrent leurs doigts fatigués
Aux replis secrets de leur robe.
Des ombres passent, ils se méfient.
Ils replacent doucement les tuiles
Et retirent les doigts de l'usure. »
Ce que tu fredonnes la Mère, n'est autre que le jus de mon rêve.
Ce qu'elle me dit fut un sirop :
« Manges donc de ma confiture, le sucre combat l'amertume.
Abrites-toi, restes sous l'if,
Gardes ta sève et ton savoir.
Méfies-toi des gestes et des fruits,
Confies-toi à moi.
Et la nuit, esquives la tentation de te confondre aux anges amers.
Choisis :
Confiture d'Or - Anges Amers - ? »

Doatea.

CLÉMENTINE, MANDARINE ET REINE CLAUDE
(Pierre BENSUSAN)

DADGAD

« Musiques » (Lost Lake Arts, division of Windham Hill, distribution : A & M)

© 1979, CÉZAME, 2 rue Flèchier, 75009 Paris, France

All rights reserved for all countries

GIGUES IRLANDAISES
(trad. Ireland ; adapt & arrgt : Pierre BENSUSAN)

DADGAD
(capo 5)

« Early Pierre Bensusan » (Lost Lake Arts, division of Windham Hill, distribution : A & M)

à Eric Schoenberg

MERRILY KISSED THE QUAKER

Moderato ♩ ≈ 112

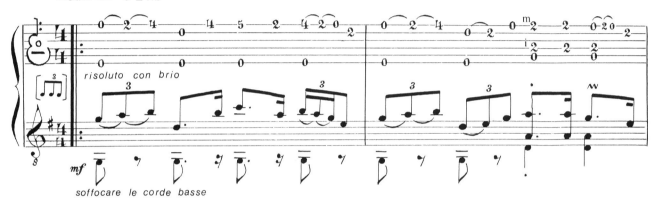

risoluto con brio

soffocare le corde basse

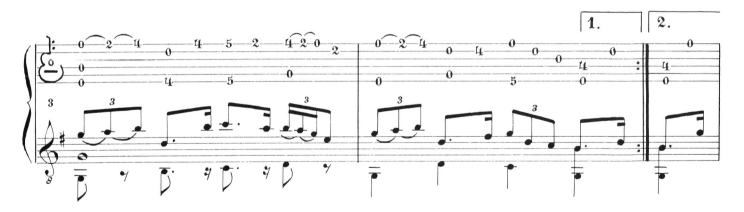

© 1984, Pierre BENSUSAN, P.O. Box 411, Mill Valley, CA. 94941. U.S.A.

All rights reserved for all countries

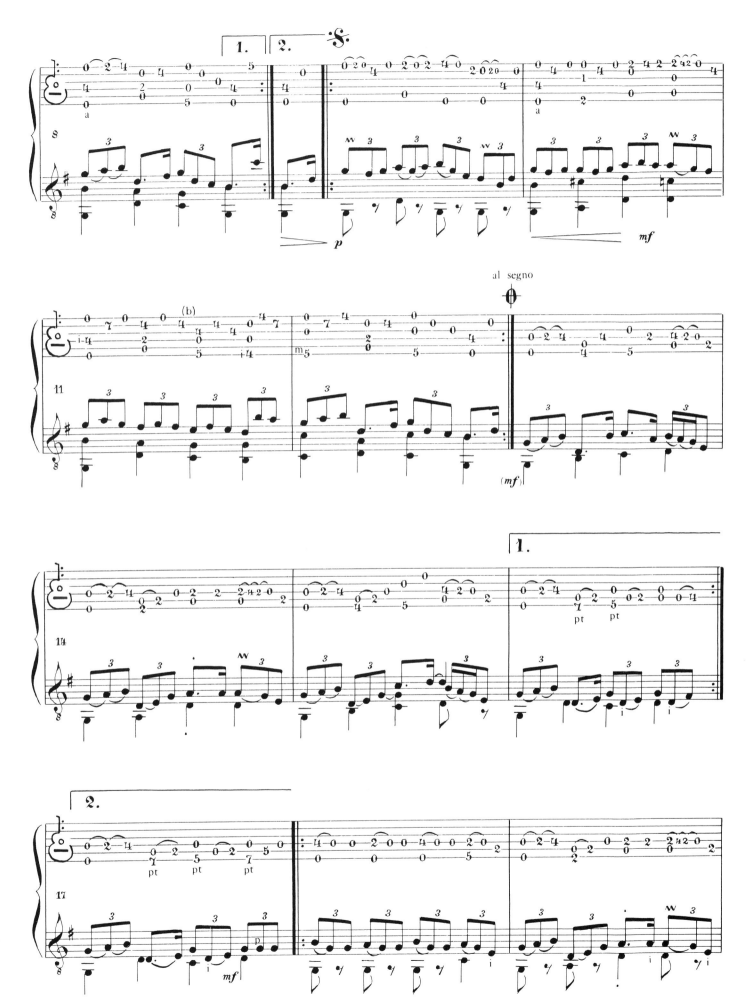

CUNLA

REELS :
THE PURE DROP /
THE FLAX IN BLOOM

(trad. Ireland ; adapt & arrgt : Pierre BENSUSAN)

« Early Pierre Bensusan »
(Lost Lake Arts, division of Windham Hill, distribution : A & M)

Seamus Ennis

© 1977, CÉZAME, 2 rue Flèchier, 75009 Paris, France

All rights reserved for all countries

The forest is a huge green chest set alongside the sea. I have always loved to rummage through the precious articles inside.

I write to you every summer to tell you about my discoveries. While the shapes have little changed, the colors are always new. In fact, I can never recreate the nuances precisely. The light needles planted along the trunk are bright green, the sun shimmers through in brief waves. The tree bark, alive, the skin of serpents is but a poor imitation. All that is missing is the play of the wind and the clouds. Bugs and butterflies, cicadas and ringdoves, a myriad of birds whose names escape me, ladybugs and glowworms, all tucked away inside, frighten me a bit.

Today, the wind picked up above the sea. It began by pushing the clouds together, then it hid the sun. Next it melted over the green chest and lightning fell. When I opened the chest, I found broken tree limbs, gnarled foliage, and dead birds piled upon wounded dragonflies.

I closed my eyes. Summer was coming to an end.

Francine Paillet

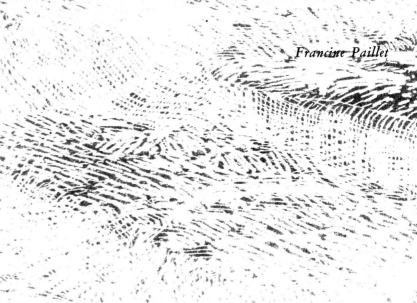

LE MOULIN A PARFUMS D'EMMANUELLE

DADGAD

(*Emmanuelle perfumes' mill*) (Pierre BENSUSAN)

« Musiques » (Lost Lake Arts, division of Windham Hill, distribution : A & M)
« Compilations » (Chant du Monde, distribué par Harmonia Mundi)

à Emmanuelle Parrénin

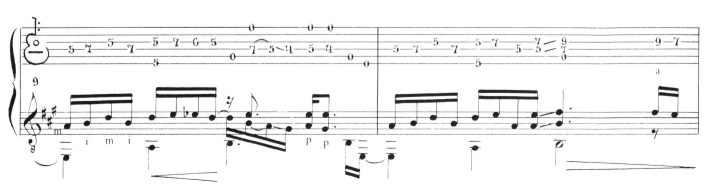

© 1979, CÉZAME, 2 rue Flêchier, 75009 Paris, France — All rights reserved for all countries

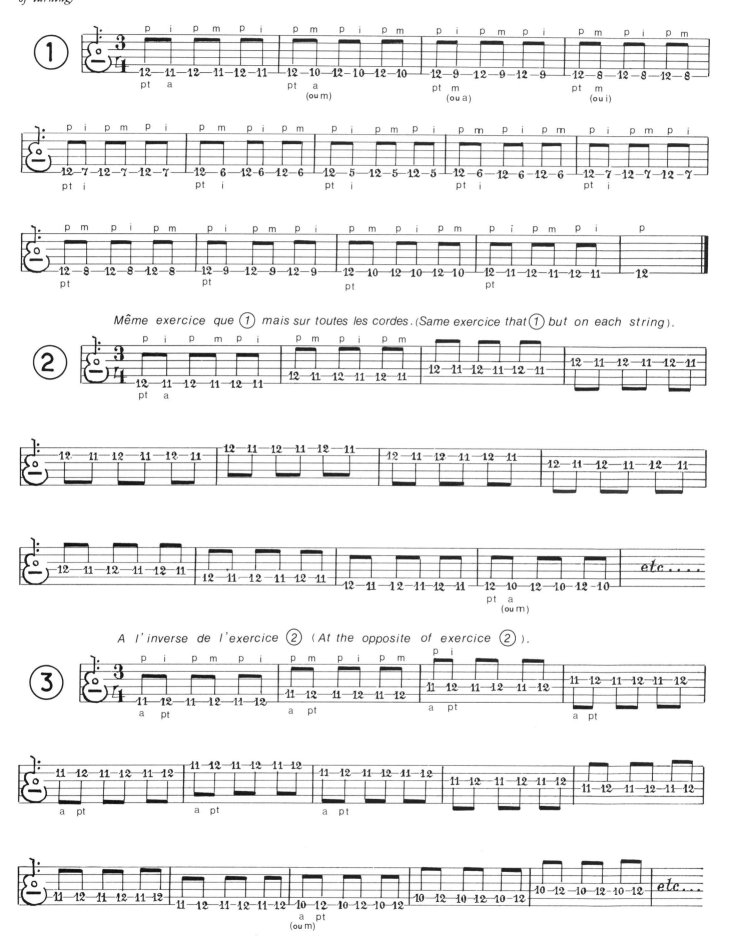

Variante de l'exercice ③

Variante de l'exercice ②

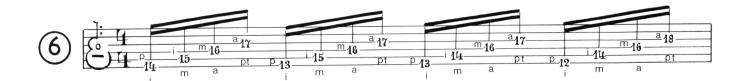

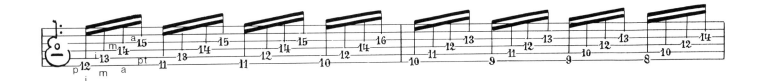

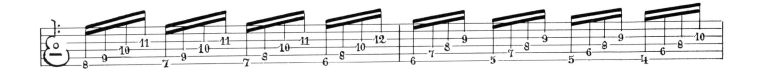

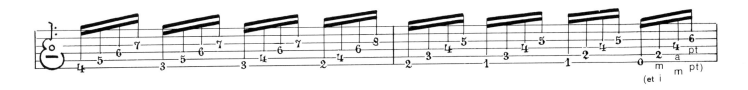

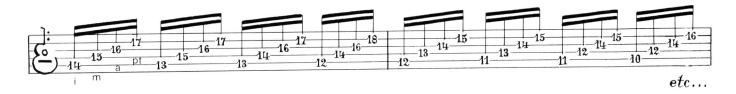

ALGERIAN SALAD (with red and green peppers).

INGREDIENTS :
(for 4)
– 4 ou 5 ripe tomatoes,
– 6 red and green peppers,
– 3 cloves of garlic, salt and pepper, and a pinch of cayenne.

Steep the tomatoes in hot water for a few minutes in order to skin them easily, cut them in half, take out the seeds, then cut the tomatoes in small pieces.

Grill the peppers, skin them, take out the seeds and cut into thin slices.

Finely chop the garlic and fry it in a pan with a tablespoonful of oil. When the garlic is browned, add the tomatoes with a pinch of salt, pepper, and cayenne. Stir from time to time with a wooden spoon.

When all the water has evaporated, add the peppers and cook for 15 to 20 minutes. The salad can be eaten hot or cold, so close your eyes and "bon voyage".

WATER MUSIC

(G.F. HAËNDEL ; adapt & arrgt : Pierre BENSUSAN)

DADGAD
(capo 3)

« Musiques » (Lost Lake Arts, division of Windham Hill, distribution : A & M)

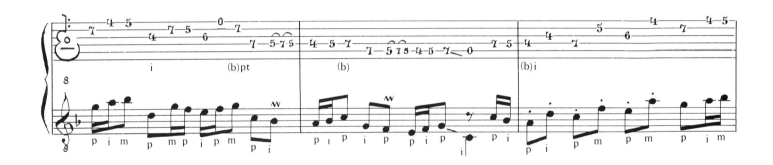

© 1979, CÉZAME, 2 rue Flèchier, 75009 Paris, France

All rights reserved for all countries

LE VOYAGE POUR L'IRLANDE
(Pierre BENSUSAN)

EADGBE

« Musiques » *(Unrecorded version)*

à Patrick Ciocca

© 1979, CÉZAME, 2 rue Flèchier, 75009 Paris, France

All rights reserved for all countries

TITOUT

« – Si tu es souris je te chasse.
   – Ce n'est pas ça que je dis.
   – Souris, ris et je t'embrasse.
 . – Si tu es pacha, souris... »

Le chat ravi,
chasse l'amante
accroupie sur le chalant, nonchalamment...
Assis le chat, la souris passe,
aguichant le félin, traînassant,
le pas lent sur la nasse.
Ni la souris jouant si tard,
Ni le chat rôdant, insomniaque,
ne savent que le charme agit.
En pas chassés, le mulot gris se carapate.
Chat se lamente : à trop faire le pacha,
le pas de chasse s'amollit.
Et, lassé de sa stratégie, de guerre lasse,
le chat se dit : « le châssis de mon char est cuit,
              point de souris, pas de pâté. »

Une souris, un chat s'enlacent,
rapetassant tout leur passé,
ils n'ont pas vu les rats voraces,
se moquant de leur hyménée,
ni en haut l'aile des rapaces
caressant l'idée de la chasse...

Doatea

SHAD AUX HERBES

Shad : a fish that swims upstream in spring to spawn.

Clean the shad one day in advance, carefully setting aside any roe.

Cut in pieces and place in a flat dish. Sprinkle with brandy and a tablespoon of tarragon vinegar or lemon juice.

Let marinate overnight.

The following day, prepare and cut fresh spinach, the green part of a bette, plenty of sorrel and new onions cut in slices.

Put a thick layer of herbs in the bottom of a dish, followed by the sliced onions and the shad ; add roe kept fresh from the night before.

Salt, pepper and finish with a bunch of herbs, bay leaves, thyme and basil.

Sprinkle with vegetable oil (olive oil if you wish). Cover and cook in medium oven for 4 to 5 hours. If possible, cook in two stages and serve with white wine.

LE LAC DES ABBESSES
(Pierre BENSUSAN)

DGDGCD
(capo 4)

« *Early Pierre Bensusan* » *(Lost Lake Arts, division of Windham Hill, distribution : A & M)*

à Gérard Charnoz

Andante

© 1975, CÉZAME, 2 rue Fléchier, 75009 Paris, France

All rights reserved for all countries

HARMONIQUES : THE FALSE KNIGHT ON THE ROAD
(trad. England ; adapt : Pierre BENSUSAN)

DADGAD

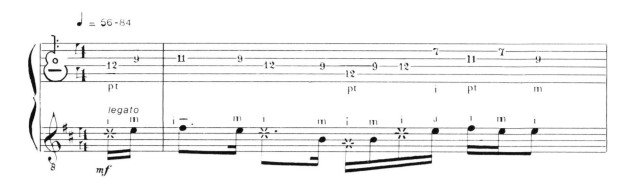
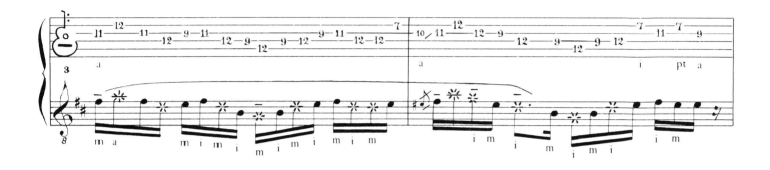
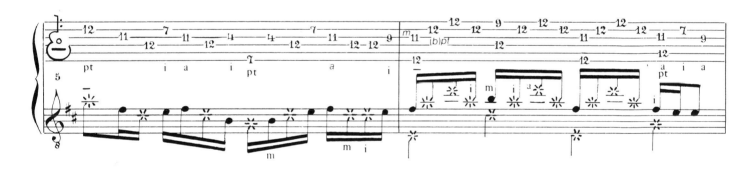
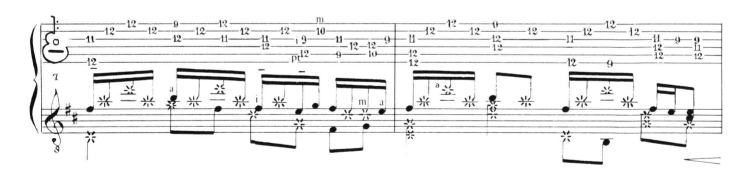
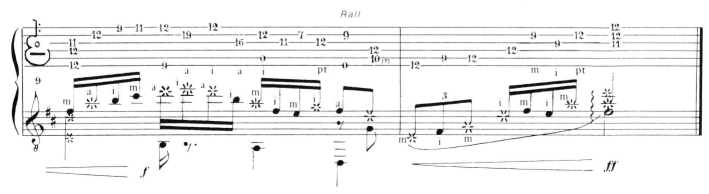

© 1985, Pierre BENSUSAN, P.O. Box 411, Mill Valley, CA. 94941. U.S.A.   *All rights reserved for all countries*

HEKIMOGLU/DIGITAL

(trad. Turkey, adapt : Pierre BENSUSAN/Pierre BENSUSAN)

DADGAD

« Musiques » (Lost Lake Arts, division of Windham Hill, distribution : A & M)
« Compilations » (Chant du Monde, distribue par Harmonia Mundi)

à Michèle Shallon

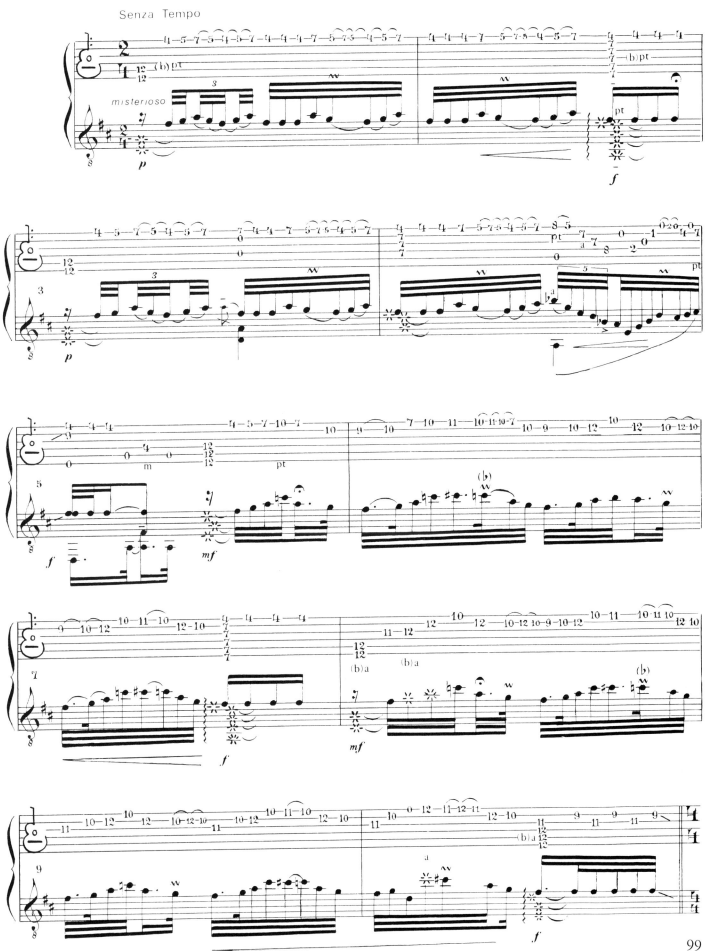

© 1979, CÉZAME, 2, rue Fléchier, 75009 Paris, France (Hekimoglu)
© 1985, CEZAME & Pierre BENSUSAN, P.O. Box 411, Mill Valley, CA. 94941. U.S.A. (Digital)   All rights reserved for all countries

CLIMATS DOUX ET TEMPÉRÉS
(for 2 guitars & voice)
(Pierre BENSUSAN)

DADGAD
(capo 2)

« Musiques » *(Lost Lake Arts, division of Windham Hill, distribution : A & M)*
« Compilations » *(Chant du Monde, distribué par Harmonia Mundi)*

à Denise Cornu

102

© 1979, CÉZAME, 2 rue Flèchier, 75009 Paris, France

All rights reserved for all countries

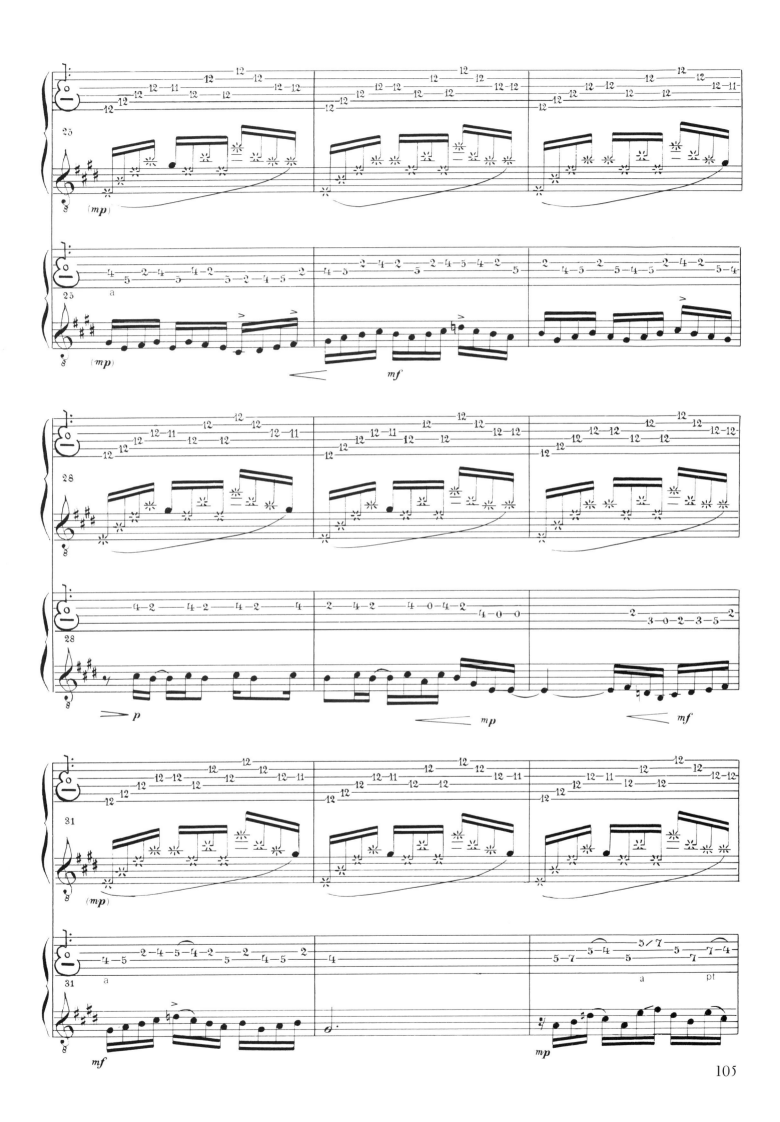

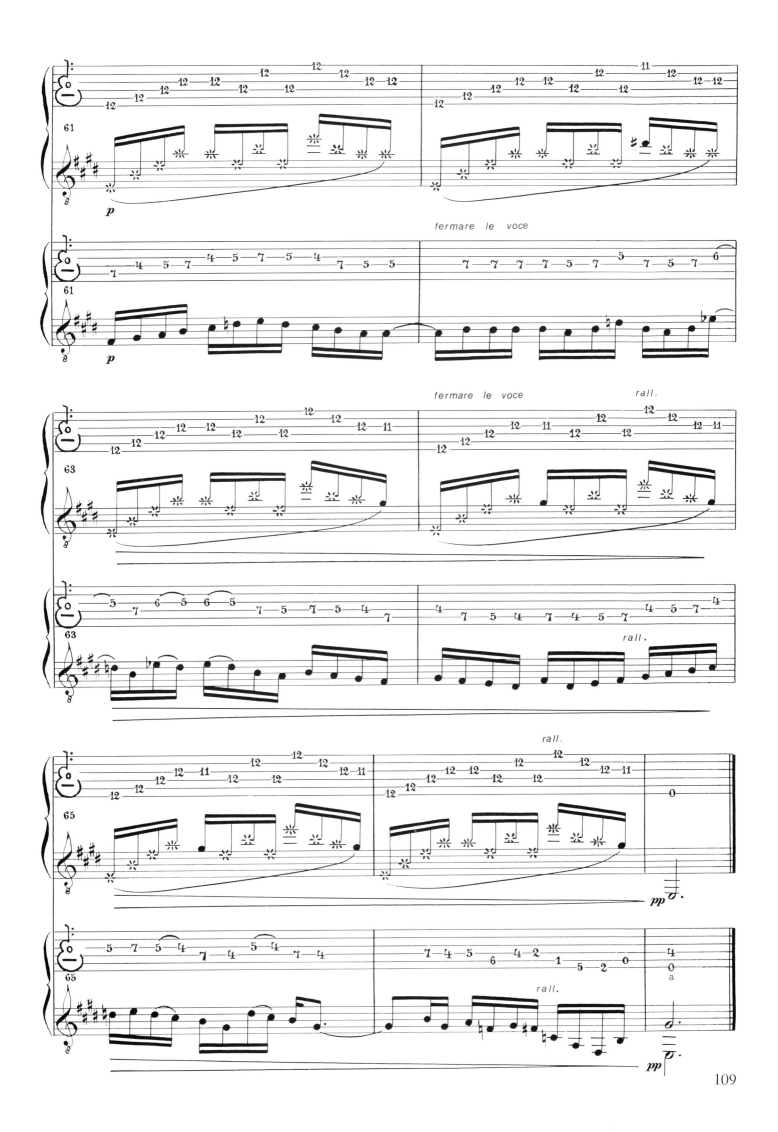

SUITE FLAMANDE AUX POMMES
(Pierre BENSUSAN)

DADGAD
« *Solilai* »
« *Compilations* » (*Chant du Monde, distribué par Harmonia Mundi*)

à Philippe Godelle

© 1982, Pierre BENSUSAN, P.O. Box 411, Mill Valley, CA. 94941. U.S.A.   *All rights reserved for all countries*

MEGUENA : a meat and vegetable pie from North Africa.

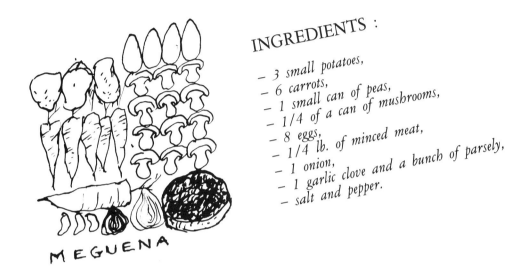

INGREDIENTS :
- 3 small potatoes,
- 6 carrots,
- 1 small can of peas,
- 1/4 of a can of mushrooms,
- 8 eggs,
- 1/4 lb. of minced meat,
- 1 onion,
- 1 garlic clove and a bunch of parsely,
- salt and pepper.

Cut the potatoes and carrots in cubes and cook them for around 20 minutes in gently boiling water.

Add the mushrooms, the onion and garlic minced finely as well as the water from the peas. Cook until the water has evaporated.

Pour the mixture into a bowl, add minced meat, peas, and chopped parsely ; add salt and pepper and break the eggs.

Preheat oven (medium).

Blend all ingredients until smooth.

Put 4 or 5 tablespoonfuls of oil in a pyrex dish and heat in oven.

When the oil is very hot, put the mixture into the dish and bake for 15 to 20 minutes.

Turn off the oven and let the mixture cool within.

Remove the pie from the dish when chilled (The Meguena is eaten cold with lemon and salad).

THE MARCH OF THE LOST PIPER

It was in Scotland, the north of Glasgow, the day of the pipers' march.
They were one hundred ; he was in the very last row on the right hand side.
He liked to feel that he was part of this wild animal with one thousand ringing bellies
and also, that he was very precisely one of the four corners of the pipers' square.
It was already late in the day and he had been marching and playing, or playing
and marching for four hours, depending on the notes and the field ;
at that moment, the piper feeling such a great unity between his steps and this music
of one hundred bellies closed his eyes to appreciate the harmony even better.
While has was doing so, the road turned on the left. The ninety nine other pipers
followed it whereas our musician of the last row went straight ahead, walking
and playing, walking, playing...
Maybe, if he finally noticed his solitude, he must have enjoyed it and prefered
wandering across fields rather than the parade lane. However, he was never to be
found again.

LA MARCHE DU SONNEUR ÉGARÉ
« The march of the lost piper »
(Pierre BENSUSAN)

DADGAD

« Musiques » (Lost Lake Arts, division of Windham Hill, distribution : A & M)
« Compilations » (Chant du Monde, distribué par Harmonia Mundi)

à Hammish Anderson

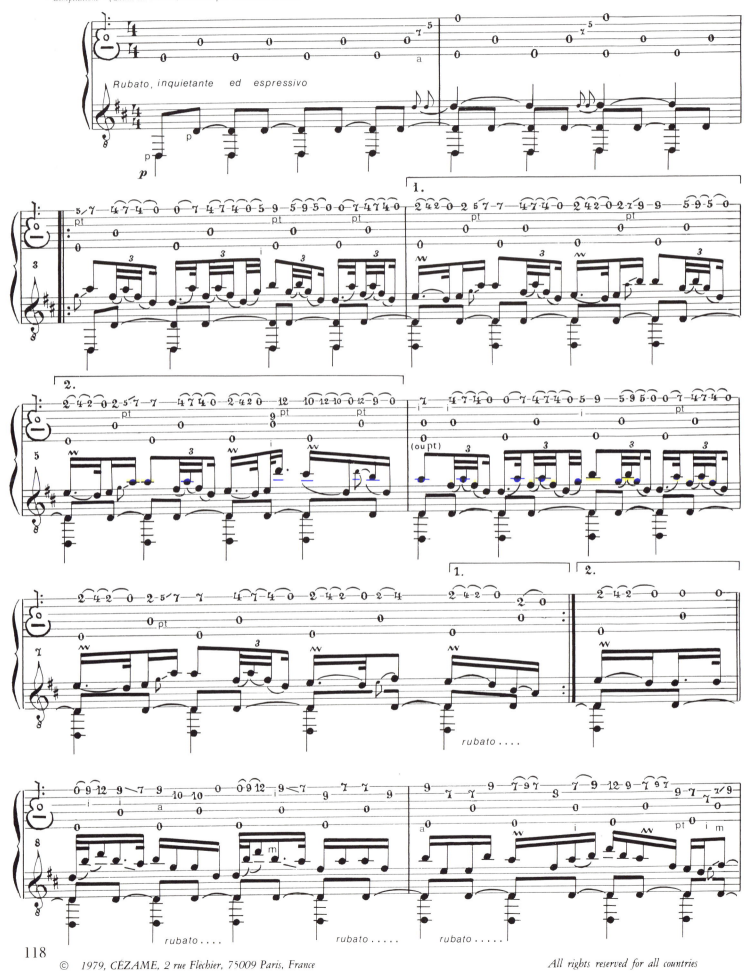

© 1979, CÉZAME, 2 rue Fléchier, 75009 Paris, France

All rights reserved for all countries

GAMME MAJEURE HARPISANTE *(mode Ionien)*
(harpisant major scale)
a. 1 OCTAVE
b. 3 OCTAVES

DADGAD

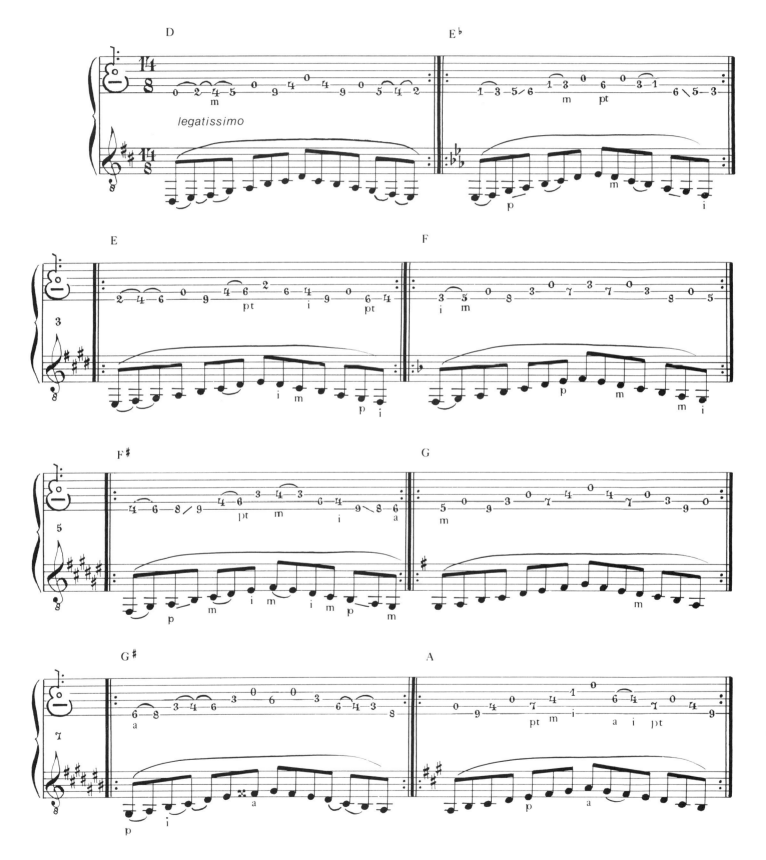

122

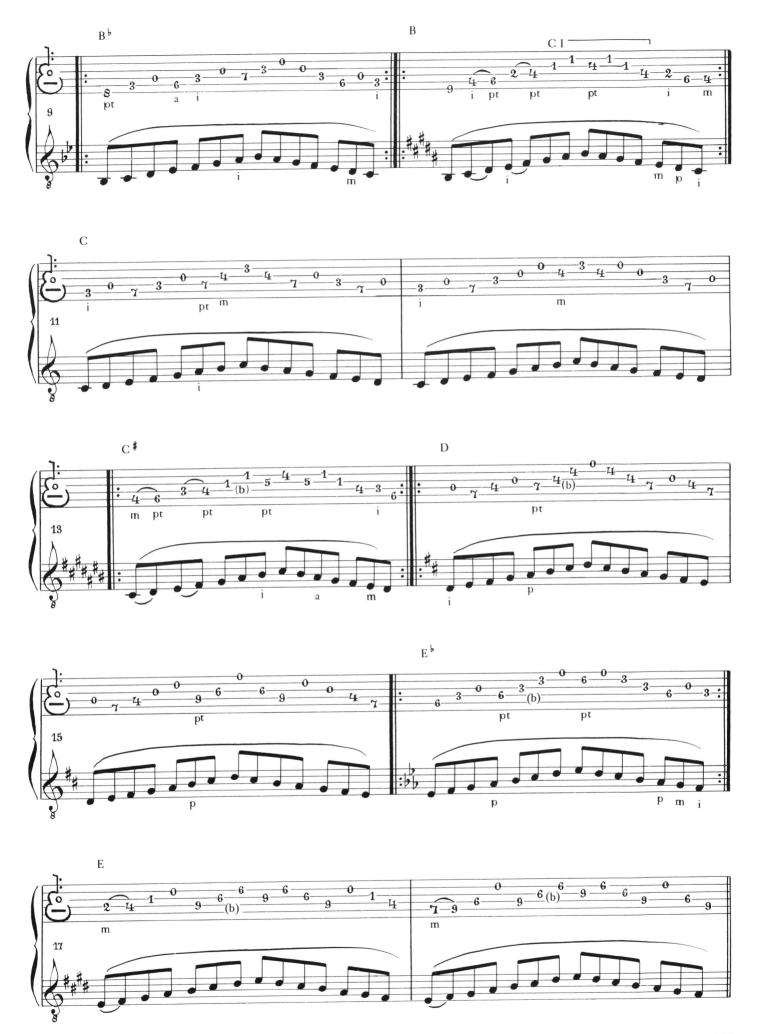

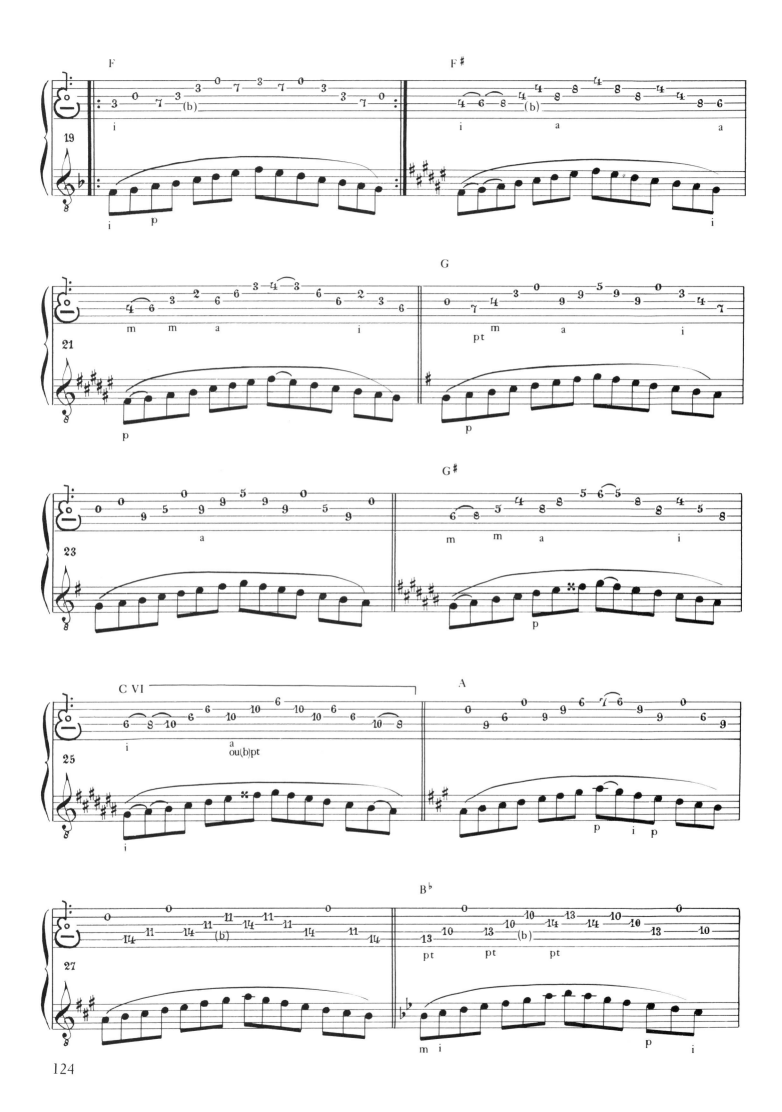

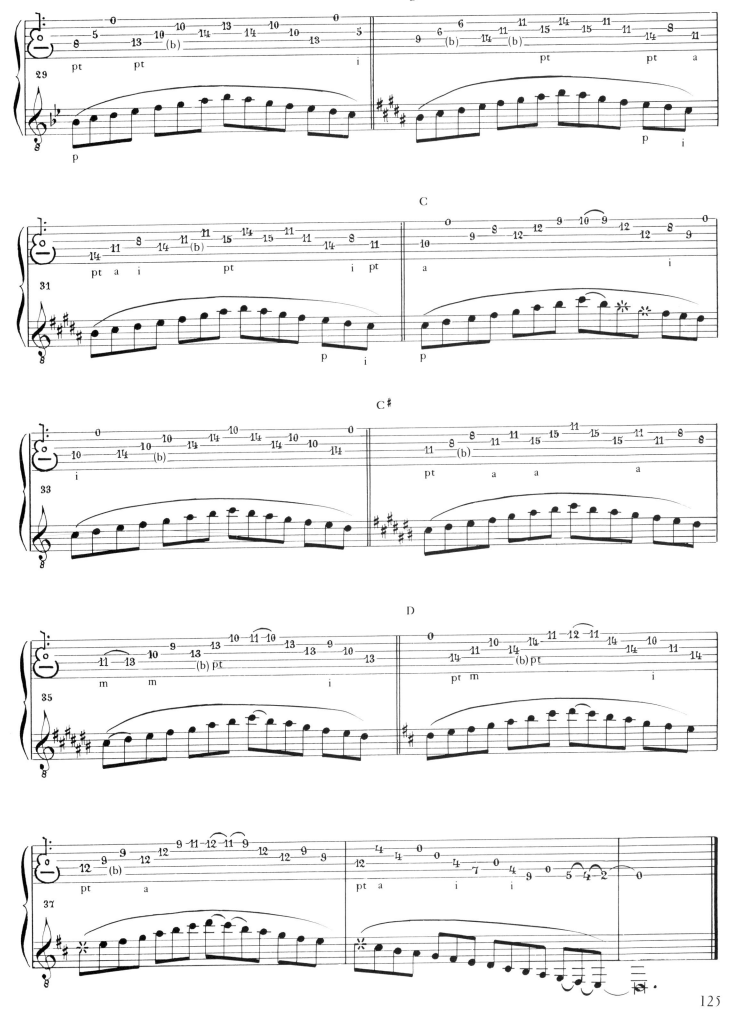

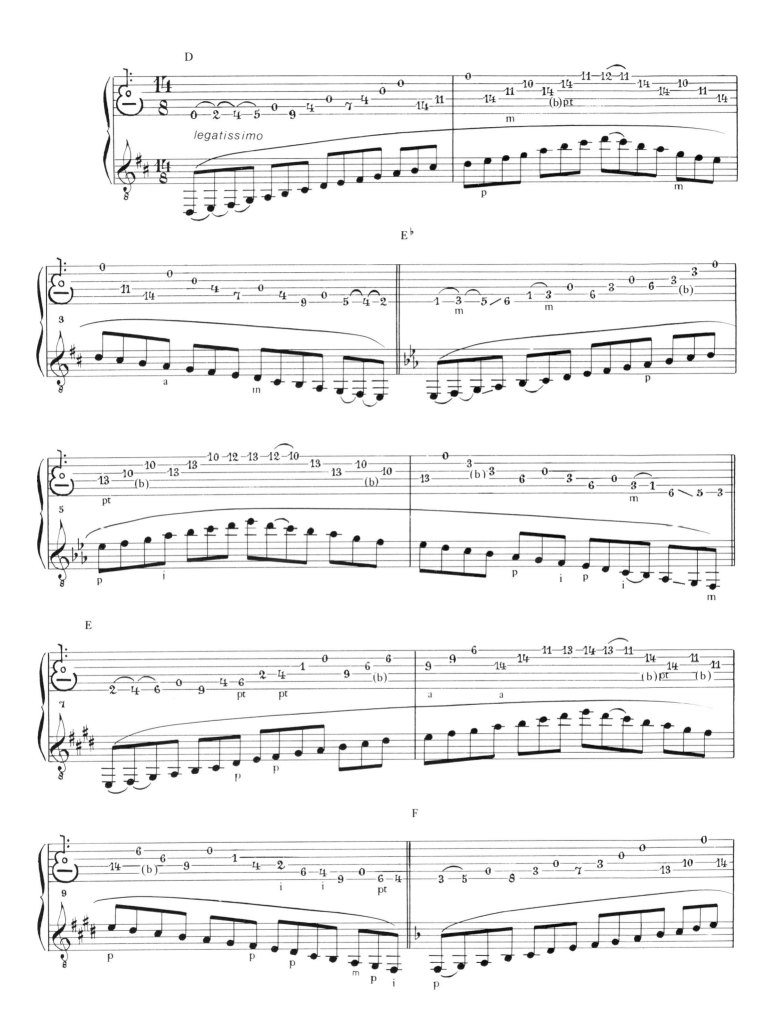

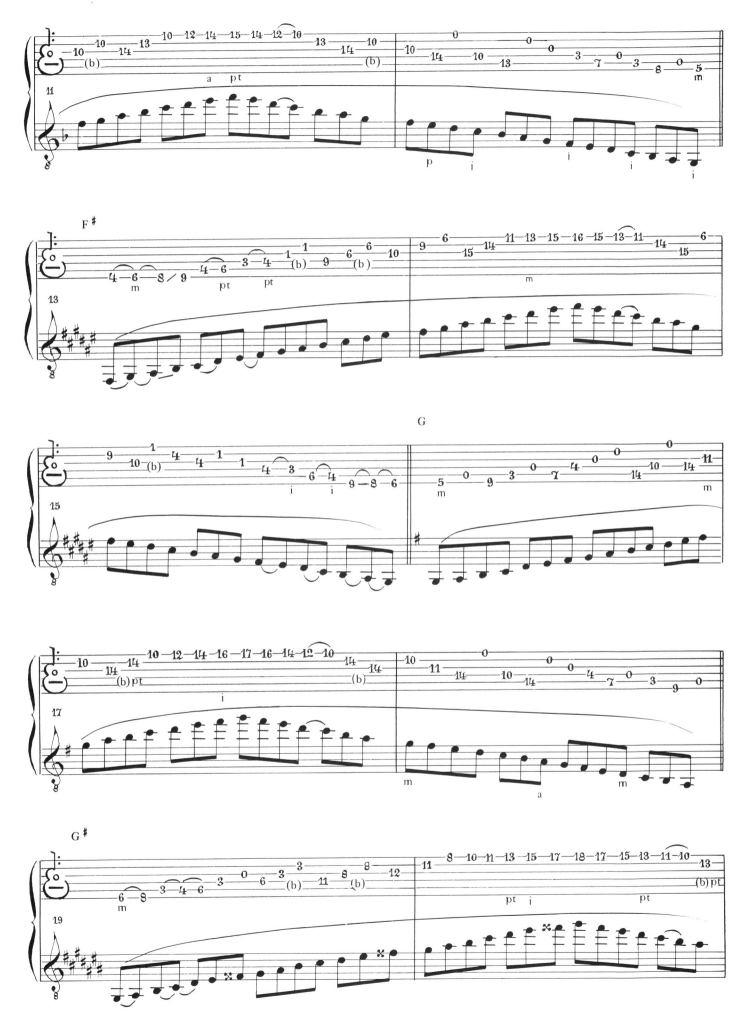

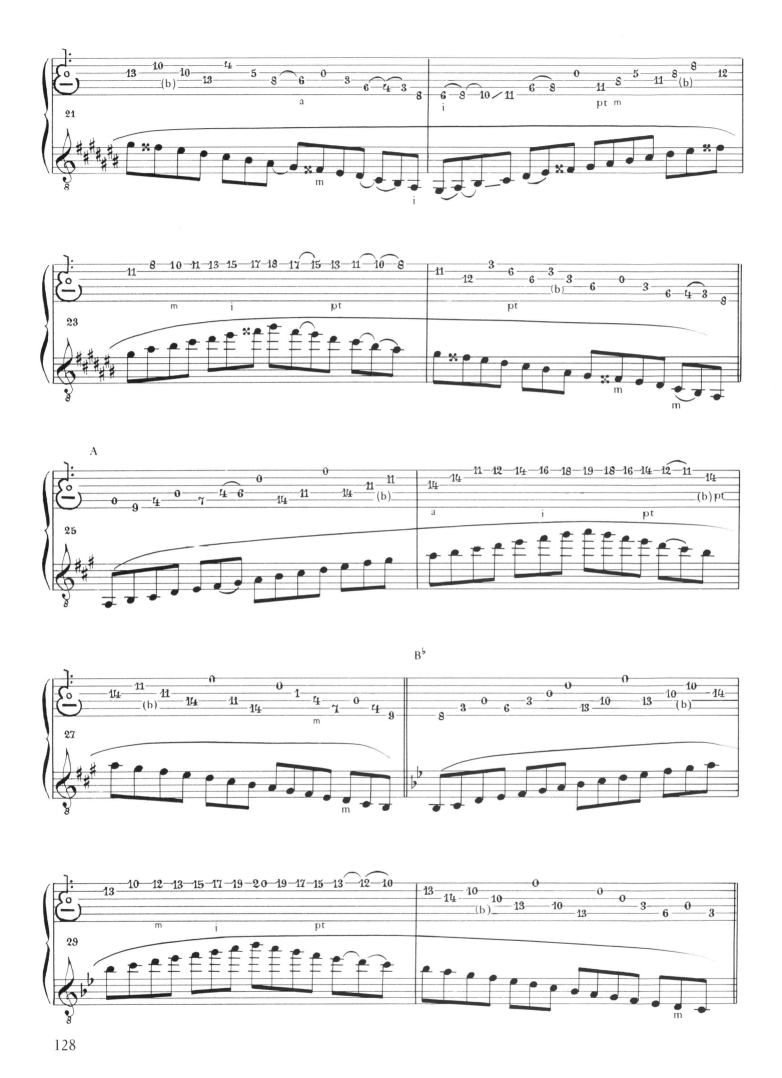

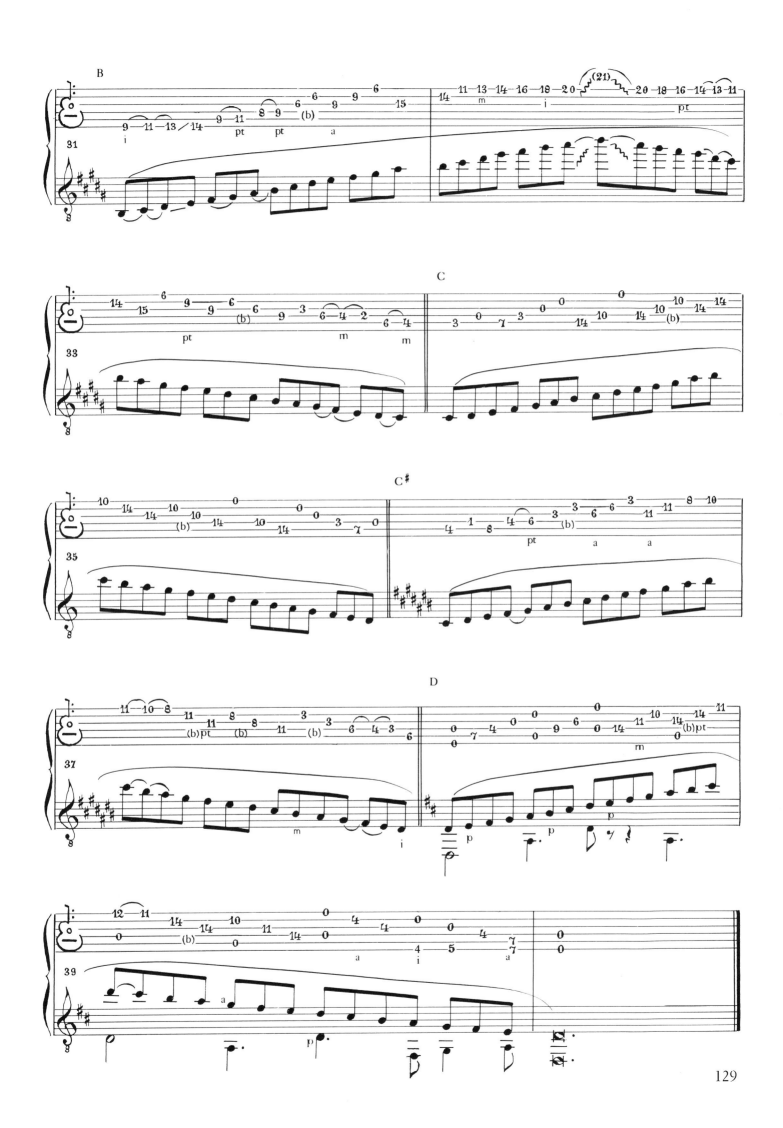

SANTA MONICA
(Pierre BENSUSAN)

DADGAD
« Solilai »
« Compilations » (Chant du Monde, distribue par Harmonia Mundi)

à Manny Greenhill

© 1982, Pierre BENSUSAN, P.O. Box 411, Mill Valley, CA. 94941. U.S.A.   *All rights reserved for all countries*

« *And you will kill your heart because it will become too difficult to live with* ».

Jean Giono

AU JARDIN D'AMOUR *(At the garden of love)*
(lyrics : trad ; music : Pierre BENSUSAN)

DADGAD
(capo 2)
« *Solilai* »

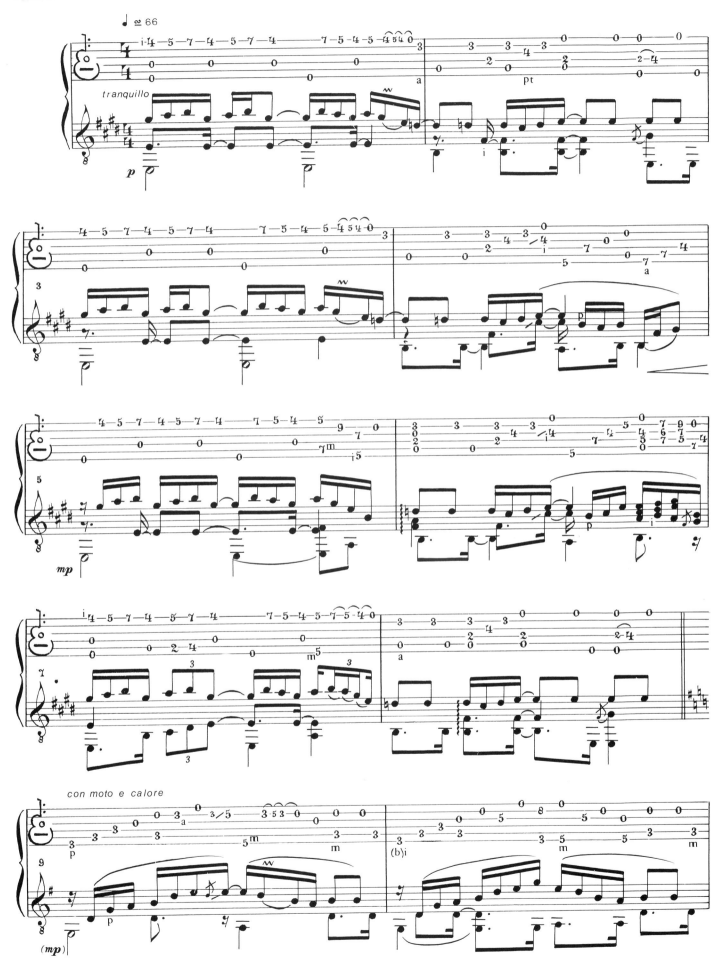

© 1977, CÉZAME, 2 rue Flechier, 75009 Paris, France
© 1982, Pierre BENSUSAN, P.O. Box 411, Mill Valley, CA. 94941. U.S.A.

All rights reserved for all countries

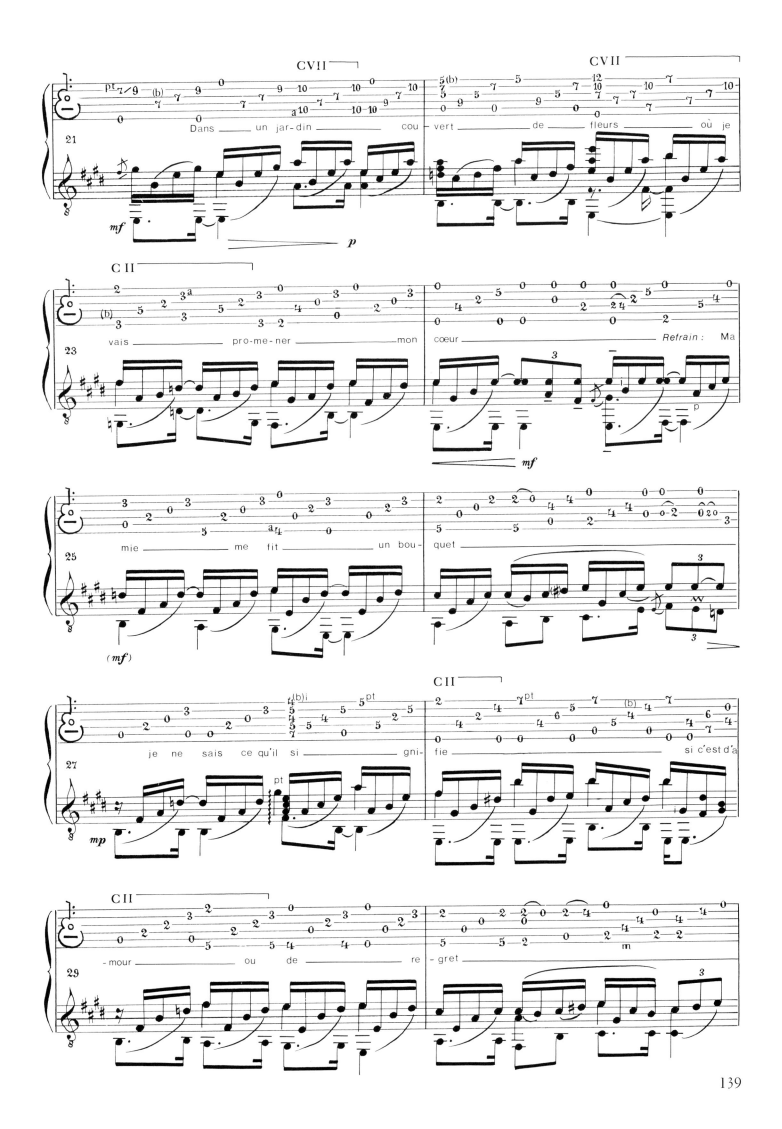

AU JARDIN D'AMOUR
(texte anonyme, XVIIIe siècle)

Jardin d'amour que tu es grand
Où je vais promener ma mie
Dans un jardin couvert de fleurs
Où je vais promener mon cœur

Ma mie me fit un bouquet
Je ne sais ce qu'il signifie
Si c'est d'amour ou de regret
ou bien pour me donner mon congé

Tous les oiseaux qui sont dans le ciel
Ne sont pas de la même mère
Ne sont pas tous pour un seul chasseur
Et ma mie pour un seul serviteur

Elle me fit un bouquet
Je ne sais ce qu'il signifie
Si c'est...

Ma mie me fit un bouquet...

LES QUATRE DANSONS

Brouillard aux abois,
Parapluies baleines,
Thé blond et gâteaux.
Les routes se creusent,
Tremblement de terre,
Prenez garde, boue, la pluie est oblique,
Les trottoirs vernis et la lune en flaque,
Tant pis, tant pis Dame
Et claquons nos bottes sur l'air de Java...

Dans les courants d'air,
Les fourrures s'envolent,
Les verres sonnent en bulles,
Les rires cascadent,
Vérandas secouant les derniers froids durs.
Les amours accourent, nos souliers se cambrent
Orion brille fort et le cœur frissonne,
Tant mieux, tant mieux Dame
Si nos yeux se frôlent, les Tangos chavirent...

Des manteaux en peau,
De nouveaux frimas,
Des buées entourent les bouches qui parlent,
Les carreaux se givrent et les feux aboient,
La forêt se livre aux sons des blizzards,
Concert de cristal et de chocolat.
Deux fruits déguisés remplacent nos yeux,
L'étoile est polaire, le froid prend nos doigts,
Accordons nos pas pour tourner la Valse...

Les nuits de tropique cachent leurs orages,
Les moustiques attaquent et l'asphalte fond,
Le front dégouline et les pieds nus glissent
Sur du chaloupé,
Entre deux cadences, je vois ton sourire
Plus que renversé.
Les lampions balancent, comètes en cavale,
Joli jeu de dames sur jungle alanguie,
Sur le pavé chaud, la Rumba ira...

Doatea.

SOLILAÏ
(Pierre BENSUSAN)

DADGAD

« Solilaï »
« Compilations » (Chant du Monde, distribué par Harmonia Mundi)

à René Matkovic

Largo maestoso, con tenerezza

144 © 1982, Pierre BENSUSAN, P.O. Box 411, Mill Valley, CA. 94941. U.S.A. *All rights reserved for all countries*

MEKRODS : small semolina cakes from North Africa
(thanks to Mrs. Lucienne Harrar & Lucette Bénita)

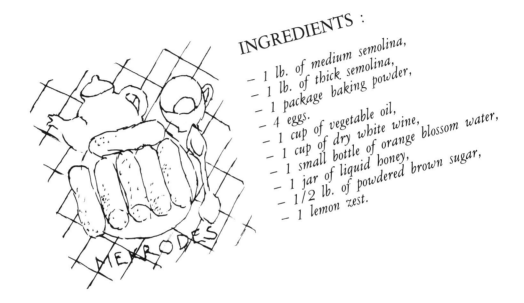

INGREDIENTS :
- 1 lb. of medium semolina,
- 1 lb. of thick semolina,
- 1 package baking powder,
- 4 eggs.
- 1 cup of vegetable oil,
- 1 cup of dry white wine,
- 1 small bottle of orange blossom water,
- 1 jar of liquid honey,
- 1/2 lb. of powdered brown sugar,
- 1 lemon zest.

Starting the day before, slightly grill the semolina and let it cool.

Mix in the baking powder and let stand overnight.

Add vegetable oil and white wine. Mix and let stand for a short time.

Beat the eggs, add the sugar and lemon zest, and mix in the semolina until the mixture is smooth.

Form dough into a rectangle (about 3/4" thick and 2" wide), cut into 1 1/2" slices, the mekrods will then be shaped and must stand for 4 hours.

Fry the mekrods at a low temperature until they are golden brown, then drain off oil.

Plunge the mekrods into a mixture of heated honey and orange blossom water so that they are well flavored.

They can be stored from 7 to 10 days in the refrigerator.

« *Sitting hunched over his guitar, Pierre Bensusan played for two hours, performing a range of music, where most often, the various styles are combined into his own sound, enchanting, mysterious and sensuous* ».

(THE OAKLAND TRIBUNE - Oakland, CA)

JÉSUS QUE MA JOIE DEMEURE

« Jesus, Joy of Man's Desiring »

(from Cantate 147 - J.S. BACH ; adapt : Pierre BENSUSAN)

DADGAD

NICE FEELING
(Pierre BENSUSAN)

DADGAD
(capo 3)

« I would say, quite honestly, that I greatly prefer that which touches me to that which surprises me ».
François Couperin

à François Allier

© 1982, Pierre BENSUSAN, P.O. Box 411, Mill Valley, CA. 94941. U.S.A.   All rights reserved for all countries

MALGRÉ LE FAUCON

Bien que le temps soit prédateur,
Et les ciels enserrés dans sa poigne rapace,
Je rends grâce à tes yeux.
Ni glaciers ni embruns, en glissant doucement
Dans les failles du temps,
N'ont forcé ton visage à retenir leurs marques.
Contre la mer il n'y a rien à faire,
Mais ton sourire traverserait mille ans de ressac.
Contre l'immuable usure, le même entêtement...
Ni glace ni embruns en glissant avec force,
N'altèrent ton visage ;
Tel un marbre chauffé par l'os de mouton,
N'acceptant que l'approche des paumes en coquille,
il ne laisse de prise qu'aux caresses concaves.
Et tes doigts, j'en augure, fabriquent pour longtemps
Des sons-fleurs tirés d'un bois riche en présages.
Si tu me dis « Viens »,
Je passerai par la Mer des Sargasses,
Mes sandales à la main, ma quête bandoulière et l'espoir sous les pieds.
L'impatience arrondie à la vue des galets,
Je plaquerai mouillées, mes empreintes durcies au velours de leur ventre.
A la faim, je ferai griller une alose contre un saule allumé.
Je prendrai le chemin des quartz ,
Où le sous-bois est feutre vert et la glaise de cire ;
L'après-midi fondra entre mes pas,
La fin du jour, plus hardi que la veille, me posera plus près des retrouvailles.
Ton appel en arceau arrêtera mon orbite,
Je plongerai entier sur toi
Dans l'élan du Faucon.

IN SPITE OF THE HAWK
(translated by the author)

Even though the talon time grips
our scratched skies,
I bless your eyes.
Neither frost or dust have touched your face.
Against the sea there is nothing one can do.
But with tenderness, your smile would cross
a thousand years of deep flux...
Neither time, nor wear and tear could ever wear your being :
against erosion, the same obstinacy.
Beyond far flowing fields, your fingers gifted with chants, I foresee,
weave blooming sounds from a rich-winded wood.
When you call me,
I shall pass the falls, sandals in hand,
on my brow my dreams, heartbeat in my heels.
I shall mark my steps wet on the river-rolled stones.
In hunger, I shall grill a trout above a burning willow branch.
Then I shall take the path of quartz where the undergrowth is felt green
and the clay honey,
feeling the afternoon melt beneath my feet.
Each setting-sun brings me closer to the day when we meet again :
Your lithe call will stop my running,
and I'll fly towards you like a hawk in spring.

Doatea.

BAMBOULE
(Pierre BENSUSAN)

DADGAD

« Solilaï »
« Compilations » (Chant du Monde, distribué par Harmonia Mundi)

« I like roots but I prefer fruits ». Caetano Veloso

à Claude Nesci et Jean-Luc Sauvaïgo

© 1982, Pierre BENSUSAN, P.O. Box 411, Mill Valley, CA. 94941. U.S.A.

All rights reserved for all countries

177

FLEMISH APPLE SUITE

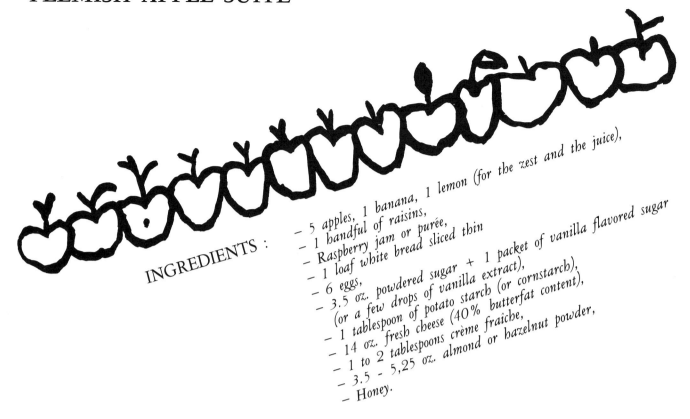

INGREDIENTS :
- 5 apples, 1 banana, 1 lemon (for the zest and the juice),
- 1 handful of raisins,
- Raspberry jam or purée,
- 1 loaf white bread sliced thin
- 6 eggs,
- 3.5 oz. powdered sugar + 1 packet of vanilla flavored sugar (or a few drops of vanilla extract),
- 1 tablespoon of potato starch (or cornstarch),
- 14 oz. fresh cheese (40% butterfat content),
- 1 to 2 tablespoons crème fraîche,
- 3.5 - 5,25 oz. almond or hazelnut powder,
- Honey.

Soak the raisins in rum or lukewarm salted water.

Peel the apples and slice them thin. Cook them in a pan with a pat of butter, a hint of cinnamon, a vanilla pod, and the juice of one lemon (after having grated off the zest). Once the apples are cooked, add the raisins (drained of their rum or water) to the apple mixture and let cool.

Using a fork and a bowl, mash the banana with 1 to 2 tablespoons of honey and the almond or hazelnut powder until a rich mixture is obtained. Add a bit of crème fraîche to bind.

Butter generously the slices of white bread and powder lightly with sugar. Cut off the edges and line them along the edges of a charlotte mold, with the buttered side against the mold, cutting the slices to fit, if necessary.

Beat the egg yolks (leaving the whites to be beaten at the last minute) with the sugar until they whiten. Add the vanilla flavored sugar, the potato starch, the lemon zest, and finally the fresh cheese and the crème fraîche beaten well together. Add to this mixture the egg whites beaten very stiff. Using a spatula, delicately lift this mixture from below in order not to break the egg whites. (Heat the oven to medium before starting to beat the egg whites so that it is sufficiently warm when it is time to put the cake in).

To keep the egg whites from falling, quickly fill the mold with successive layers of raspberry purée, apple mixture, the cheese/cream mixture, and then the nut mixture, starting with a thin layer of purée, a layer of apple mixture, a layer of nut mixture, then another layer of apple mixture and the rest of the cheese/cream mixture, and so on, covering the top with a layer of white bread.

Bake for 35 to 45 minutes. Check for doneness with the tip of a knife : the knife should come out clean and the bread should be golden brown. Let cool in the oven with the door open and remove the charlotte from its mold when warm or cool. Place in a hollow dish.

The « Flemish apple suite » should be eaten with custard cream, beaten crème fraîche, or fruit purée while listening to the Flemish Apple Suite (Suite flamande aux pommes).

DOCTOR GRADUS AD PARNASSUM
(Claude DEBUSSY ; adapt : Pierre BENSUSAN)

CADGAD

© 1984, Pierre BENSUSAN, P.O. Box 411, Mill Valley, CA. 94941. U.S.A.   *All rights reserved for all countries*

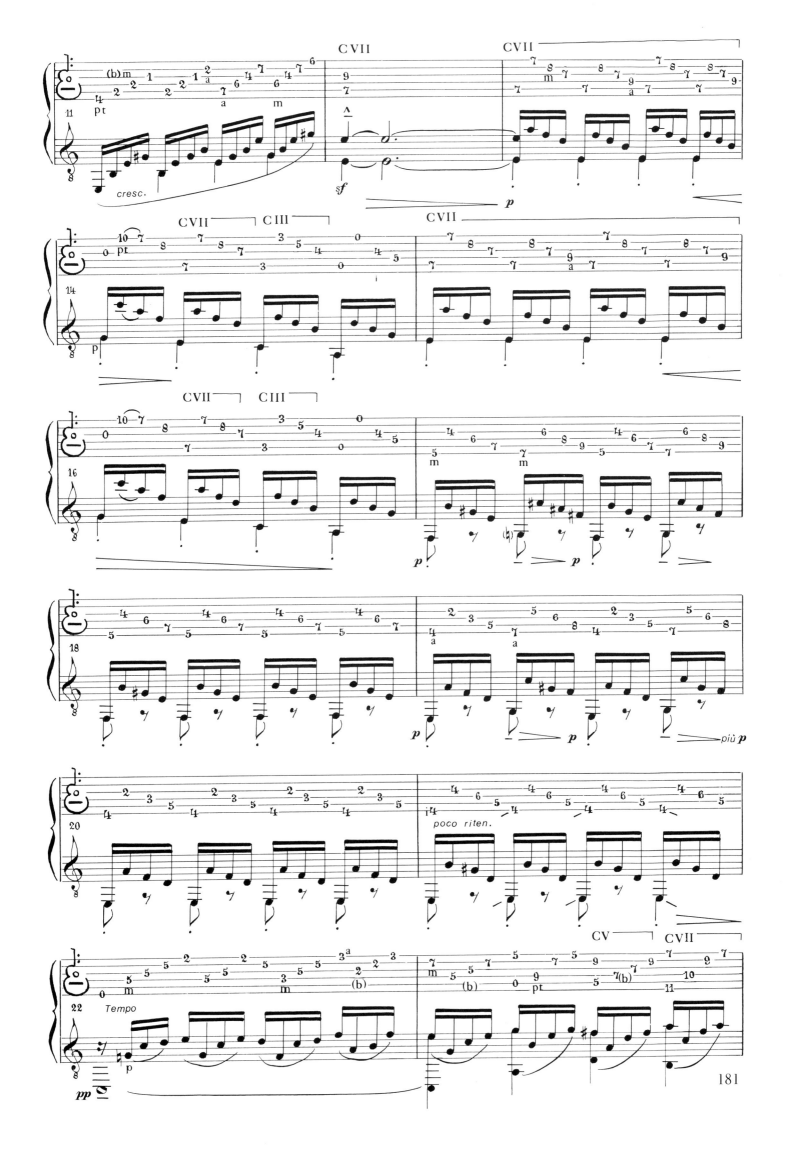

René Coste, calligraphe.

ABOUT THE AUTHOR

« Superb balance between the nostalgia of the Renaissance and the most modern swing ».
(LE SOLEIL DE QUEBEC, Canada)

Pierre BENSUSAN has been described as « a poet of the guitar », « a natural », « a wizard of sounds »...

Born in Algeria in 1957, Pierre came to Paris with his family in 1962. At the age of seven, he began to study classical piano. Some years later, however, he chose the guitar which he taught to himself. He finished school at the age of sixteen, and the following year he recorded his first album which was awarded the Grand Prix du Disque at the Montreux Festival.

This musicien brings together the influences of many periods and countries, transcending them individually to create an original style of personal expression which brings to light his Mediterranean roots. A remarkable solo interpreter (Bach, Debussy...) he composes for electroacoustic guitar and voice, as well as for groups. He concertizes the world over.

« Superlative imagination and technical skill, one of the best testimonials yet for the remarkable range of the acoustic guitar ».
(ACOUSTIC MUSIC, U.K.)

« Mr BENSUSAN measures every detail of tone, articulation and counterpoint in pieces that covered a lot of geopgraphy. The sounds he makes are ravishing. A rare elegance ».
(THE NEW YORK TIMES, U.S.A.)

« A music articulated brillantly, with rhythmic impetus that is compelling ».
(THE GUARDIAN, London, U.K.)

« A Musician's musician »
(THE IRISH TIMES, Dublin, Eire)

« Poet of music, his sonority on the guitar is enough to make him one of today's great guitarists. Four encores... he could have kept playing for hours ».
(NICE-MATIN, France)

LIST OF RECORDINGS

« Early Pierre Bensusan » « Musiques » (Lost Lake Arts, Windham Hill division, distribution : A & M Records - U.S.A. - Canada - Japan et POLYDOR - Europe) « Solilaï » (C.B.S Masterworks)

Notes by Bob GILES.

Illustrations

Pierre Bensusan, photograph by Lisa Law	p. 2
Drawings by Patrick Alexandre	p. 8-9
Nice « promenade des anglais » photograph by Philippe Steger	p. 4
Photograph of a Marocan musician by Yvon Kervinio	p. 14
2nd Maghreb music Festival (Nanterre 1985) Drawing by Vincen Cornu	p 20
Photograph by Billy Riley	p 21
Drawing by Vincen Cornu	p 22-23
Anatomic and warm-up sketches drawed by Patrick Alexandre	p 24-25
Photograph by Jennifer Linehan	p 32
Photograph by Lawrence Perquis	p 33
Photograph by Loïc Tréhin	p 34
Photograph by Lawrence Perquis	p 35
Photographs by Philippe Steger	p 43-51
Ink drawing by Loïc Tréhin	p 55
Photograph by Jacques Barberi	p 65
Ireland, photographed by Daniel Cariou	p 72
Drawing by Loïc Tréhin	p 76
Photograph : courtesy of Claddagh Records (Dublin)	p 79
Engraving by Loïc Tréhin	p 82-83
Pierre Bensusan at the 1983 Quebec Summer Festival, photograph by André Pichette	p 89
Photograph by Philippe Steger	p 94
Lake Geneva (Switzerland), photographed by Nicky Gygger	p 96
Engraving by Loïc Tréhin	p 101
Venice, Italy, photograph by Philippe Steger	p 110
The Cat in Toulouse, photographed by Michèle Nédélec	p 117
Santa Monica, view from the "Sea Castle", photographed by Doatea	p 132
Wood engraving by Bruce Harris	p 136
Pierre Bensusan, photograph by Lisa Law	p 153
Algeria, photograph by Philippe Steger	p 166
India, photograph by Philippe Steger	p 179
Pierre Bensusan photographed by Irene Young	p 186
Technical photography by Loïc Tréhin	
Recipe illustrations by Vincen Cornu.	

Table of contents

Acknowledgments	p. 5
Preface	p. 6
Introduction	p. 7
GLOSSARY	p. 9 to 43
Amplification	p. 10
Arpeggiated chords	p. 10
Arpeggios	p. 11
Attacks - Nail care	p. 12
Bars, Partial bars	p. 17
Capo	p. 18
Caring for the guitar	p. 18
Fingerings	p. 19
Glissando	p. 20
Guitar Making	p. 21
Glossary of Italian expressions	p. 22-23
Hands and body position	p. 24
Harp effect	p. 28
Interpretation	p. 28
Musical notation	p. 29
Natural harmonics	p. 30
Poem by Gérard Cornu	p. 31
Open strings	p. 32
Pauses	p. 33
Rubato	p. 33
Short history of the guitar family	p. 33
Singing	p. 35
Slurs, ornaments	p. 36
Strings	p. 37
Tempo, movement, metronome	p. 39
Thumb-pick	p. 40
Vibrato	p. 40
Culinary interlude : Pumpkin soup	p. 44
The return from Fingal	p. 45
Exercises : Arpeggios (Arpèges)	p. 46
Interlude : Four grain bread	p. 49
Le voyage pour l'Irlande	p. 50
Poem by Doatea : "Amani"	p. 51
The Rakkish Paddy	p. 52
Le lendemain de la fête	p. 54
Poem by Francine Paillet	p. 55
Près de Paris/Reels	p. 56
La danse du Capricorne	p. 58
De Trilport à Fublaines	p. 60
Exercise : the harp effect	p. 63
Heman Dubh	p. 64
Maurice au pays des merveilles	p. 66
Poem by Doatea : Fine parabole de l'amère confiture d'orange	p. 69
Clémentine, Mandarine et Reine Claude	p. 70
Irish Gigs : Merrily kissed the quaker/Cunla	p. 72
Murtagh Mc Kann	p. 76
Reels : The pure drop/the flax in bloom	p. 79
Poem by Francine Paillet	p. 82
Le moulin à parfums d'Emmanuelle	p. 84
Exercise : stretches/Attacks	p. 86
Interlude : Algerian salad	p. 88
Water Music	p. 90
Le voyage pour l'Irlande (second version)	p. 92
Poem by Doatea : Titout	p. 94
Interlude : Shad aux herbes	p. 95
Le lac des abbesses	p. 96
Harmonics exercise : The false knight on the road	p. 98
Digital/Hekimoglu	p. 99
Climats doux et tempérés (for two guitars)	p. 102
Suite Flamande aux pommes	p. 111
Interlude : Meguena (North-African recipe)	p. 116
La marche du sonneur égaré	p. 117
Exercise : major scales with harp effect	p. 122
La petite et la grande colline (Si Bhig, si Mhor)	p. 130
Santa Monica	p. 132
Au jardin d'amour	p. 137
Poem by Doatea : les Quatre Dansons	p. 143
Solilaï	p. 144
Interlude : Mekrods (North-African pastries)	p. 152
Jesus, Joy of Man's Desiring	p. 154
Nice feeling	p. 158
Poem by Doatea : Malgré le faucon	p. 166
Bamboulé	p. 167
Interlude : Suite Flamande aux pommes	p. 178
Doctor Gradus ad Parnassum	p. 180

« Music should make a humble effort to please ».

Claude Debussy

First Edition February 1986
English Edition February 1987

LE LENDEMAIN DE LA FÊTE
(The day after the feast)
(Pierre BENSUSAN)

EADGBE

« Early Pierre Bensusan » (Lost Lake Arts, division of Windham Hill, distribution : A & M)

à Hervé Delors

© 1977, CÉZAME, 2 rue Fléchier, 75009 Paris, France

All rights reserved for all countries